GRASS FARMING

GRASS FARMING

M. McG. COOPER

C.B.E., D.Sc. (Massey), B.Agr.Sc.(N.Z.), Dip.Rur.Econ. (Oxon),
B.Litt. (Oxon), F.R.S.E., F.R.A.S.E.

Formerly Dean of Agriculture, University of
Newcastle-upon-Tyne

and

DAVID W. MORRIS

B.Sc. (Wales), Ph.D. (Dunelm), F.R.Ag.S.

Principal, Welsh Agricultural College,
Aberystwyth

FARMING PRESS LIMITED
Wharfedale Road, Ipswich, Suffolk

First published 1961
Second impression 1962
Second edition (Revised) 1967
Third edition (Revised) 1973
Fourth edition (Revised) 1977
Second impression 1979
Fifth edition 1983

© FARMING PRESS LTD 1961/77

ISBN 0 85236 140 8

This book is set in 11pt on 13pt Times Roman
and printed and bound in Great Britain
at The Camelot Press Ltd, Southampton

CONTENTS

CONTENTS

PLATES

FOREWORD

by A. S. CRAY, MBE, JP

Since Professor Cooper gave us *Grass Farming* in 1961, the farming scene has undergone important changes. In their Preface, the authors of this revised edition have called attention to several of them.

They mention the great advances in technology and in the management of pastures and grazing animals, and there is of course significant improvement in the returns from beef and sheep as compared to milk. Ability to exploit the grass crop is vital to enable us to be competitors in the Common Market, to fill the gap caused by reducing imports of meat and animal products and to meet the needs of an increasing population.

It is still the position that efficient grass production and utilisation is the most complex of our agricultural activities. The comparison between the tillage crop and the grass crop which was made in the Foreword to the 1961 edition still holds good. With the tillage crop the management of the single plant is simple compared with the grass crop, where it is usual to grow two or more varieties together. Each has a different growth habit and each is responsive to or is depressed by certain treatments at certain times. A treatment beneficial to one may depress the other. The crop is growing and is being harvested intermittently or continuously over a long period, with consequent difficulty of accurate assessment of annual yield. Dealing with these challenges is what grassland management is all about.

In this edition the authors have dealt with virtually all the circumstances that arise in the day-to-day and year-to-year management of grassland of all types. Even more important perhaps, they have covered these features of animal management that are related to the successful conversion of grass, fresh and conserved, to meat and milk. Failure in this final stage means failure of the whole enterprise.

It has long been apparent that the loss of nutrients in conservation as hay or silage is the outstanding weakness of our grassland husbandry. The need is for a method of conservation that approaches the efficiency of grass drying but at lower capital cost. The authors call attention to the heavy nutrient losses involved in the making of silage and hay but they have given detailed guidance on keeping these losses to a minimum.

Farmers will appreciate particularly the farming language used throughout this book and the clear-cut separation of the various aspects of their subject. This, and the clear indexing, add greatly to its value as a practical handbook to be referred to time and again after the first reading.

Professor Cooper and Dr Morris are to be congratulated on their success in bringing up to date a book on this all-important subject. It will be welcomed and appreciated by an ever-growing number of farmers and farm managers who have come to realise the potential of the grass crop.

Roe Downs Farm,
Medstead
Nr Alton
Hants
May, 1973

PREFACE

When the senior author prepared the manuscript for the first edition in 1961, entry into the Common Market was no more than a distant and uncertain prospect. Now it is a reality and British agriculture is facing a challenge at least as great as that created by the Second World War. But in 1939 British farming was in poor shape. Millions of acres had either gone out of effective production or were in low quality permanent pasture, but today the lands of Britain are in good heart and there is a level of technology that compares favourably with that of any country in the world.

In particular, there has been a tremendous advance in the management of pasture and in the handling of grazing animals. Though agricultural scientists have contributed to these advances, unquestionably the major contribution to the rise in the general level of grassland husbandry in Britain is attributable to progressive farmers that can be found in almost every county in this country. We have in mind men like Sam Cray in Hampshire, Ted Owens in Somerset, Edwin Bushby in Cumberland, Oliver Barraclough in Yorkshire (on difficult millstone grit that would break most people's hearts) and Maitland Mackie Junior in Aberdeen. These are but representative names of the many who have convinced their fellow farmers that pasture is green gold if it is properly handled. It is to men like these that this book is dedicated and also to the memory of that very great agricultural scientist, Sir George Stapledon, who back in the thirties realised before any of his contemporaries the importance of good grassland husbandry in the entity of British farming.

We would like to thank everyone who has helped us in the preparation of this book. We cannot mention each one by name but we would be most ungrateful if we did not say 'thank you' to Senorita Teresa Caro Santa Cruz and Mrs Beryl Morgan for deciphering our untidy long hand to put it into shape for the typesetters. Our long-suffering spouses – the wife and daughter of the senior author – also deserve a mention because authorship imposes such restraints on family life.

M. McG. COOPER   D. W. MORRIS

PREFACE TO FIFTH EDITION

It is ten years since the last revision of *Grass Farming* and a decade is a long time in a period of rapid technical and economic change. Membership of the EEC and the unprecedented levels of inflation that the United Kingdom has experienced since 1972 have altered completely the relationships between costs and returns. These conditions have also affected the amount of capital required to buy and stock a farm, which has now reached staggering proportions. Land that would have been considered dear at under £500 per acre in 1970 is now changing hands at five times that figure and prices for fuel and agrochemicals with a petroleum basis have gone through the roof. There have been substantial increases in commodity prices but on the whole cereal growers have been more fortunate than livestock producers, especially those in pigs and poultry who are suffering because of the current high prices of feeding grains. Those with ruminant livestock are in a more favourable position because grass in its various forms is still the cheapest food for cattle and sheep and there is still a lot of scope on the average farm for increasing the effective take-off of grass nutrients.

Ironically, fat lamb production is presently the most promising sector of the livestock industry, after a long period of stagnation, even regression, during the almost-forgotten era of guaranteed prices and February price reviews when sheep were the Cinderellas of farming. Now that we are in Europe and some measure of agreement has been reached with our French partners in CAP on exports to that country, there has been a substantial rise in the price of lamb. This combined with a better understanding of the environmental factors affecting flock performance, is making intensive fat lamb production a much more attractive proposition than it has ever been in this century. On the other hand, despite technological advances as well as substantial increases in the selling price of milk, the future of dairying is less favourable than it was in its immediate past. The reason for this is the so-called milk lake and though domestic production is unable to meet the United Kingdom's requirements for milk and milk products we are part of the Community and its surplus is also our surplus. It is possible that the dairy industry may be subject to quotas in the not too distant future and if this happens dairy farmers may find it uneconomic to press for high yields with heavy concentrate inputs. It may be better for them to put a greater reliance on grass and accept lower yields per cow in what will essentially be a low-cost system of dairying.

A book such as this is not written just by the names that appear on the title page – the work and thinking of many people have contributed to its contents, including those whose help was acknowledged in the previous edition on which this one is substantially based. We are grateful to Beryl Morgan and Hilary Cooper for their secretarial assistance in what has not been a very straightforward job. With the wisdom, some would say the cunning that comes with age, we asked a younger man who has kept abreast of recent advances in this area to revise the chapters on herbage plants and grass seed mixtures and we greatly appreciate the help that Dr John Harries has given us in this connection. If it is wisdom, we hope that a large measure of it has been distilled on to the pages that follow to the benefit of those who read this book and make a living from land and livestock.

M. McG. Cooper   D. W. Morris

Chapter 1

THE IMPORTANCE OF PASTURE

Pasture is the most important single crop in British agriculture. In its various forms, short and long leys and permanent grass, it accounts for nearly two-thirds of the cultivable land and, in addition, there are approximately 6·8 million hectares of rough grazings which make an important contribution to output in an area where there is a critical shortage – namely, the production of meat. When the history of British agriculture is written to cover that dynamic period which started in 1939, and which one hopes will not come to an end, the contribution of these so-called rough grazings will be really appreciated. In recent years there has been criticism that too much money, mainly in the form of Government subsidies, has been put into the upland sector where most of the rough grazings are to be found, but lowland farming in Britain, and the British housewife too, would be in a much worse position were it not for the contribution that these marginal areas make to the nation's food supplies.

If there has to be criticism about upland farming, in our opinion it would be better directed to the failure to put the necessary research effort into the betterment of these lands to achieve a fuller realisation of their production potential. Unquestionably they have a very much greater contribution to make in terms of feeding cattle and store sheep now that we are facing the reality of life in the Common Market.

Foresters may say that this land has another function but no one has yet looked critically at the economics of afforestation and compared them with the more immediate results that can be obtained by a sensible input of capital and technical know-how into the improvement of this land for livestock production. The continued rise in the value of lowland farms puts our uplands into a totally new perspective and though it can never be land that will produce high priced crops it can make a very vital contribution to meat supplies, now that a sirloin steak is as expensive as fresh salmon.

LOWLAND GRASS

We must not, at this early stage, let our enthusiasm for the uplands and their developmental problems obscure the importance of lowland grass – the 2·3 million hectares of rotational grass and the 5 million hectares of permanent grass that account for such a significant proportion of total agricultural production. There was a time, and we will be referring to this topic in greater detail later, when permanent grass was regarded as a term of abuse, and great endeavours, mainly in the form of generous ploughing-out grants, were made to reduce its extent. These grants substantially failed, not because the carrot was insufficiently attractive, but because of a general realisation that permanent grass, when it is properly managed, can be just as productive as leys and is generally a cheaper source of nutrients than temporary grass. Particularly is this true on heavy land where the soil can lose structure when it is under the plough. Under these conditions too, permanent grass is especially valuable, in comparison with short-term leys, when there is high intensity stocking because damage from poaching can rapidly become a limiting factor to productivity.

Apart from their contribution to the extension of the grazing season, the greatest contribution that leys make in British agriculture lies in the effect they have on yields of arable crops under a system of alternate husbandry. There is a very limited range of soils in Britain, mainly brick earths and silty loams, where continuous arable cropping can be maintained without serious detriment to yields. A few years ago, in a vain endeavour to simplify farming and to reach the happy situation of a five-day week, except at times of pressure like seeding and harvest, a large number of farmers turned to continuous cereal growing on land that was manifestly unsuited for such management.

Unfortunately they had the encouragement of advisory services which had been bitten by the bug of gross margins and capital was re-deployed from an investment in stock into machines and equipment which are a rusting and wasting asset. Yields on which optimistic forecasts were based started to fall because of soil structure problems, an increased incidence of perennial weeds, pests and diseases. An alarmed Ministry of Agriculture, isolated from farming by the bricks and mortar of Whitehall, and characteristically behind the times in its appreciation of the problems of the industry, set up a committee to report on this loss of yield and profitability which was aggravated by two very difficult seasons – a bad harvest followed by a catastrophic spring for clay-land farmers, who also had to suffer the effects of a severe summer drought.

Out of this, and the reporting committee could do little more than reiterate the sound premises on which alternate husbandry is based, came a realisation of the importance so far as a large area of lowland Britain is concerned of maintaining a sensible balance between pastures and crops. But pastures cannot be justified solely because of their contribution to succeeding tillage crops. They must, as the rental value of land rises, make their own positive contribution to farm profitability and herein lies the importance of a proper understanding of how to manage and exploit rotational grass.

CHEAP SOURCE OF NUTRIENTS

Even in those halcyon years before we joined the Common Market, when barley cost less than £25 per tonne and high protein cake sold for about twice this figure, pasture was the cheapest source of nutrients for ruminants, always providing farmers were capable of managing their stock to make optimum use of their grassland. Despite the vast lift in concentrate prices and returns for animal products this situation has changed very little and successful ruminant livestock production in Britain will continue to depend on an intelligent exploitation of this country's pasture potential.

In this respect its compares more than favourably with all the other countries of the Community with the exception of the Atlantic seaboards of France and Eire. This latter country is in a highly advantageous position, as far as grassland farming is concerned, except for the congenital incapacity of the average Irish farmer to take life seriously. British farmers will only have real cause to fear the competition of Irish grassland when Dutchmen and Danes as well as Irishmen discover the new El Dorado that Ireland offers because of its substantial climatic advantages.

The truly continental areas – the heartland of France and Germany and most of Italy – are not well suited to pastoral production as we know it in Britain. Maize and lucerne, apart from wheat and barley, are the crops best suited to their climate and there is a big future for these once the Continentals resolve their farm structure problem. This is where we in Britain have an enormous advantage. Admittedly, we still have too many farms that are too small, in the context of a modern society that demands a herd of at least 60 cows or 750 ewes per labour unit to be economically viable, but we also have a preponderance of the farmed area of Britain in units of sufficient size to give this country a competitive advantage. Additional to these natural and structural advantages over the Continental countries, there is the British flair for stock management. British farmers generally are good stock-men and this is especially true the further one goes north or west in these islands. One cannot come to any other conclusion than that British farming will continue to have a highly competitive future for its grazing livestock because of the productivity of its grassland.

COMPLEMENTARY FUNCTION OF CONCENTRATES

Many grassland enthusiasts, and the senior author of this book has not been guiltless in this respect when he was younger and less temperate in his views, have extolled the virtues of pasture without a proper recognition of its limitations. These stem from two principal deficiencies; first, seasonal differences in productivity from mid-spring plenty to the winter trough, and second, the qualitative changes that occur over the grazing season. When pasture is at its best, in that leafy stage in early May, when it has the characteristics of 'a watered concentrate', there is no immediate advantage to be derived from supplementation except perhaps to ensure an adequate intake of magnesium. But a very different situation exists over the greater part of the year in Britain, especially in dairy production where a judicious use of concentrates will pay dividends.

Our situation in this respect differs very much from that in New Zealand, which is generally regarded as the world's leading pastoral country. Because of a favourable climate New Zealand has a very long growing season and farmers there have evolved efficient systems of seasonal milk and lamb production that are based entirely on pasture utilisation. Their returns from milk and lamb in relation to the cost of cereals are such that it simply does not pay to supplement pasture. Their example is valuable to British farmers in that they have a well-established confidence in the value of well-managed grass in achieving a high level of output per hectare. This was something the average British farmer had to learn because up till a few years ago he remembered a time when concentrates were cheap, and fortified by advertising pressure from the provender trade, he continued to think of pasture in terms of maintenance plus 10 to 14 litres of milk. Even today there are tens of thousands of dairy farmers who continue to feed appreciable quantities of dairy cake in the month of May when grass is at its best. If they get as much as an additional litre of milk for every kilogram of supplement fed, they will be getting a better than average return but they will not be making any profit.

So far as dairying is concerned, the aim must be to provide high quality grass over as long a grazing season as is possible under the natural conditions of a farm. One must aim to conserve surplus grass before it deteriorates nutritionally and also to adopt methods of conservation that minimise nutritive losses. But having done all these things, there will still be a need, especially with an autumn calving herd, to use concentrates judiciously in order to get the best out of one's grassland. The position will be different with a spring calving herd or with fat lamb or beef production, but here again a sensible use of supplements can pay dividends. This is a point we will return to later in this book.

PRODUCTION AND PROFIT

When considering production, whether it is milk or meat, it is unwise to think only of individual yields because the law of diminishing returns applies just as much in the feeding of livestock as it does in the fertilising of crops. There are two main components that contribute to livestock output per unit area under grazing conditions. The first is the individual performance of animals in terms of milk production or liveweight gain and the second is stocking intensity. There is a conflict between these two components in that beyond a certain critical intensity of stocking, individual production tends to fall. However, it is well established that maximum yield per hectare is not coincident with maximum production per animal. In other words, in the interests of a fuller and a more economic use of pasture nutrients, we can afford to sacrifice some measure of individual yields when we increase stocking intensity to its optimum level. For instance, under a system of set stocking we may produce 18 fat lambs per hectare, weighing 22 kg dressed weight apiece, but with forward creep grazing on the same area we could produce thirty lambs each weighing 18 kg. The management problem is always one of achieving the best relationship between stocking intensity and individual output to achieve the optimum economic results.

It is this sort of situation that makes grassland farming such an intriguing study. Obviously no good farmer likes to lose out on individual output if he can possibly avoid doing so, and the general inclination is to do everything one can to make the best of two worlds. If a farmer is sensible, he gradually increases his stocking intensity but then, to counter losses in individual productivity, he adopts all those measures that safeguard individual productivity – higher levels of fertilisation to increase output, better control of grazing to ration supplies and safeguard quality of herbage, better conservation methods, a more judicious use of supplements and so on.

There is no better spur to a more efficient utilisation of pastures than having a hungry herd or flock breathing down one's neck because when you are in this situation, and you have a conscience as well as an anxious bank manager, then you really start to do something about your pasture management.

Chapter 2

CHOICE OF GRAZING ANIMAL

Dairy cows are our most efficient grazing animals in the sense that they produce the greater quantity of saleable products and the greater monetary return per unit area in comparison with either sheep or beef cattle. It is primarily for this reason that dairying is practised on expensive land and especially on smaller farms. Indeed on a farm of less than 35 hectares it is questionable whether the rearing of replacements is justified, for usually it is preferable either to buy point of calving heifers from a reliable source or, alternatively, to arrange for contract rearing of selected home-bred heifer calves.

There are several reasons for this comparative superiority of the dairy cow under circumstances that demand high intensity production. On the whole, meat production is a comparatively inefficient biological process when measured in terms of food conversion. Even under good management beef cattle are only about half as efficient in turning their food into human food as dairy cattle under comparable conditions, when one takes the contribution of calves as well as milk output into account. In Britain, as well as in other countries of Western Europe, where there is such a pressure on land resources, the contribution of dairy-bred calves, surplus to breeding needs, is becoming increasingly important in beef production because the overhead cost of producing these calves is carried by milk production. It is for this reason that a truly dual-purpose breed like the Friesian is so important in Britain.

Though there is generally less capital invested in a beef-breeding cow as compared with a dairy cow, and though the latter has a greater food requirement, nevertheless the total value of production of the dairy cow, taking both milk and calf into account, is far in excess of that obtained from the suckler cow which has only two products – its calf and such subsidies as governments may provide. Admittedly the labour input, with its double daily grind of milking, is very much higher with dairy cattle than it is with sucklers. On small family farms though this is not a serious economic restraint because a farmer is usually prepared and able to put time into his dairy enterprise, since it gives him a much better living than any alternative use of his land.

Even on large dairy farms, with a mainly hired staff, the labour cost per litre has not kept pace with the rise in wages because of the quite remarkable increase in labour efficiency that has characterised the British dairy industry over the past two decades. That long succession of innovations – improved milking parlour designs, quick milking, circulation cleaning, bulk collection of milk, mechanisation of conservation, self-feeding of silage, cubicle housing and mechanical handling of slurry, to mention some of the more important developments – have made an enormous difference to labour efficiency and unquestionably this has contributed to the stability of the dairy industry.

DAIRYING MORE ADVANTAGEOUS

Another very important advantage of dairying over meat production, which stems from the relative efficiency of dairy cattle, lies in the greater scope that a dairy farmer has for using both fertilisers and purchased concentrates. The use of concentrates with beef cattle or sheep must be sparing, with existing price relationships and limited to periods of critical importance; for instance, late pregnancy and the early stages of lactation in the breeding ewe or the final fattening stage with bullocks where a concentrate supplement is an essential addition to a mainly silage diet if the desired rate of gain and degree of finish are to be attained. Certainly in winter milk production, no matter how good he is in respect of the quality of his conserved grass, no farmer can expect to get optimum economic performance from his herd without some feeding of concentrates. Apart from their direct contribution to yields they also have the effect of increasing the total carrying capacity of a farm. In a sense, when a dairy farmer buys concentrates he is adding hectares to his farm and in the process, provided these concentrates are used to good effect, he is achieving economies of scale.

NITROGEN USAGE

The same applies in the use of fertilisers, particularly nitrogen. If a farmer relies entirely on lime, phosphate and potash to maintain a balanced clover-grass sward, he will be fortunate to achieve a dry-matter output of 6,500 kg per hectare. The application of 350 kg of elemental nitrogen, provided there is sufficient moisture, can boost dry-matter production to 11,000 kg or more per hectare. But this boost in production and the utilisation of this additional nutriment costs money. Apart from the actual cost of the fertiliser, there is also the need for closer subdivision and more sophisticated control of grazing as well as improved standards of conservation.

The greater efficiency of the dairy cow can justify these costs but there is no evidence that this is the case either with suckler cows or stores that are being finished on pasture. The latter are slow to finish on grass-dominant swards that are the inevitable result of high nitrogen usage. Their best performance is generally on swards with a considerable clover content.

Generally, one can conclude that apart from dressing pastures for enhanced conservation crops, and possibly for early bite and back-end grazing, the feeder and breeder of beef cattle has a very limited scope for using nitrogen. The situation, however, is different in the eighteen-month system of beef production where autumn-born calves, at a stage when they are relatively efficient food converters, are growing frame during their summer on grass. Here there is considerable justification for high nitrogen usage, combined with controlled grazing, and the conservation of grass surplus to immediate grazing needs. With this system one must think in terms of about four beasts to a hectare of grass, and this level of stocking is not feasible unless one is using at least 200 kg of elemental nitrogen per hectare each year.

Conventional fat lamb production, based on a summer stocking intensity of 10–12 ewes per hectare plus their lambs, and some cattle grazing to control surplus grass, does not in our experience justify a heavy use of nitrogenous fertilisers. Again, as with feeding cattle, there is a better finish on the lambs if there is a strong clover element in the sward, but the situation is rather different under a system of forward creep grazing where one is able to run 20–25 ewes plus lambs per hectare. Here the aim is not lambs fat off their mothers, except in the case of singles, but forward store lambs for subsequent finishing, or possibly for immediate sale where we export lambs to Continental Europe, which requires a leaner carcass than that in demand in Britain. Fourteen years of experience with forward creep grazing on the University of Newcastle's Nafferton Farm indicate that the opportunist use of nitrogen to preserve a good sequence of grazing over the summer is an economic proposition. Certainly, an average summer output in excess of 900 kg liveweight per hectare could not have been obtained if there had been a complete reliance on clover nitrogen.

One further advantage of dairy production over both beef and fat lamb production must be mentioned and this relates to cash flow. Admittedly, the dairy farmer has a much higher investment per hectare in the form of livestock, buildings and equipment and there are also larger outgoings for labour, fertilisers and feeding-stuffs, but there is also the monthly milk cheque and often the now substantial return from surplus calves sold at the week-old stage. The suckler man has to wait nine months for his annual cheque if he sells his calves as weaners, and if he elects to finish them as young beef, there will be at least six further months before the money goes into his bank account. The situation of the eighteen-month beef producer, buying week-old calves, is even more difficult because he has to buy another crop of calves and incur substantial early rearing costs before the first bunch has been sold. At its peak the total investment per hectare for an intensive eighteen-month system can approach that of dairying.

RELATIVE ADVANTAGES OF SHEEP AND CATTLE

Normally in Britain one finds sheep in association with cattle rather than as a sole enterprise. There are several reasons for this. On upland farms, traditionally used for sheep production, there was a move to cattle because Government policy during the fifties and sixties was, through the medium of preferential headage subsidies, directed towards an expansion of beef production. By comparison sheep have been the Cinderellas among livestock but since the mid-seventies the situation has changed dramatically and sheep farming has at long last achieved a reasonable buoyancy.

On lowland farms there is age-old belief that under high intensity stocking a sheep's worst enemy is another sheep and that it is important to dilute the grazing hazards, particularly those arising from parasitic worms, by bringing in another species of grazing animal. There is good evidence from many sources to show that mixed stocking does, in fact, reduce parasitic infection of lambs so that the widespread practice of associating cattle with fat lamb production has real justification if other more positive methods of controlling worm infections are not adopted.

There have been considerable advances in this connection in recent years as a result of the availability of more efficient drugs and a better understanding of the life cycle of the more important parasitic worms. Through a combination of strategic dosing and field hygiene it is possible to maintain a high intensity of stocking within a season on the same field with a negligible worm problem, provided that the field in question has not carried ewes and lambs in the previous year. The safest fields in this respect are maiden seeds but the same effect can be obtained by conservation and cattle grazing in alternate years as a means of disinfecting pastures that have been subjected to heavy sheep stocking. It is important, however, to drench ewes against the 'spring rise' in worm egg output before they go on to clean pasture because undrenched ewes can lay down a significant level of infection that will impair late summer thrift in their lambs.

The possibilities of a greater intensity of fat lamb production, using more fecund ewes, have been greatly enhanced by these developments. With the growth in demand for meat in the world at large, and particularly in Western Europe, and the severe limitations on any great expansion in breeding cattle numbers, really intensive fat lamb production could have a new dimension in Britain which, apart from Ireland, is the only country in the Community that has any effective organisation for such production. After ten years in the Common Market and some resolution of the problems of exporting lambs to France there is manifestly a considerable upward turn in sheep-meat production in Britain, which is largely at the expense of specialised beef production.

SHEEP AND CATTLE TOGETHER?

To return to sheep and cattle in combination, there is a
widespread belief that when the two are run together there is
a fuller use of grass and a greater production per hectare
than that obtained when either species is grazed separately.
Cockle Park supplied some evidence many years ago that
there is greater production from sheep and cattle than there
is from sheep alone. This conclusion was not based on any
planned experimentation but from observations of performance on two adjacent fields. Anyone knowing the land in
question and the rates of stocking that were adopted would
be bound to conclude that there was a considerable measure
of under-utilisation, particularly on the sheep alone enclosures which were under-stocked.

More comprehensive trials at Ruakura in New Zealand
comparing breeding ewes alone, cattle alone, and ewes and
cattle in combination, under conditions of full utilisation
revealed no appreciable differences in meat production per
hectare. The expectations are that if this trial were repeated
in Britain, and the necessary precautions were taken to
control disease, the sheep alone treatment would be the
more productive and in the absence of any discriminating
subsidies the more profitable.

There are several reasons for advancing this view. The
first is that British lowland ewes, which are mainly first
crosses with a Border or Blue faced Leicester male parent, are
much more fecund and deeper milkers than the Romneys used
in the Ruakura study, which would not produce more than
18 kg of dressed lamb per ewe as compared with at least 32 kg
for a British cross-bred ewe. Secondly, longer and more severe
winters in Britain impose a much greater strain on cattle as
compared with New Zealand conditions. It is admitted that
British ewes also suffer a harder winter than their counterparts in New Zealand, but sheep as a species have a much

better adaptation to the ups and downs of pasture production over the course of the year.

This especially is true of breeding ewes because maximum food demands coincide with the greatest abundance of pasture during the late spring and summer. Weaning, and the subsequent sale of lambs or their removal to feeding crops like rape and soft turnips takes a burden off pastures as they start to fail, while the normal autumn flush provides that rise in the plane of nutrition immediately prior to mating, which is so important in securing a good lamb crop. It is only in that period, immediately prior to and just after lambing, when better feeding is essential for these highly prolific ewes.

Add to the argument these points – there is the wool by-product which despite the competition of synthetic fibres still makes a significant contribution to farm income. Then there is a better cash flow from the ewe flock than from a herd of breeding cows. In addition, there is an appreciably lower investment per hectare in breeding stock than there is with a herd of sucklers.

Lamb and mutton in Britain has had to face much more competition from imports, principally from New Zealand, than has been the case for beef as a consequence of a reduced international trade in this latter commodity. It is true that there is a world shortage of beef and this is likely to continue. Because it is a preferred type of meat it is unlikely that there will be any slackening of demand but lamb, provided it is not over-fat, is also a meat with a strong potential demand, particularly in those Continental countries where it is now a luxury food. When one sees the prices being paid for what we could consider to be miserable undersized lambs in the south of France or in Northern Italy then one realises the tremendous market potential that exists for British sheep farmers in the expanded Community, especially when New Zealand supplies are limited by tariffs and the direct subsidies for domestic beef production are largely absorbed in the market return.

UPLAND FARM EXPANSION

As lowland sheep production is dependent to a very considerable degree on the supply of breeding and store stock from both hill and marginal farms, it is important that the output of sheep is greatly increased from these two sectors of British farming. Indeed, with the very high cost of good farming land there are strong grounds for advocating a greater output of fat lambs from marginal rather than from good lowland farms, where a sheep flock can only be an economic proposition if it has a secondary role as an integrate of a more intensive system of land use such as cash cropping.

Expansion of sheep flocks on both hill and marginal land should not, however, be completely at the expense of cattle production, for there are distinct management advantages in maintaining a reasonable balance of sheep and cattle under these conditions. Apart from the point already made that an association of cattle and sheep, as opposed to sheep alone, reduces the challenge that the flock has to face from parasitic worms, there is the improvement in the quality of sheep grazing that results from the judicious use of cattle, particularly where it is not possible because of contour to control pastures by topping. There are many examples in Britain of upland farms that have been greatly improved by the introduction of cattle and one of the great, and sometimes unrealised benefits of Government endeavours to get more beef from hill and marginal land, has been the vast improvement that has been effected in the quality of its pastures since 1950. In New Zealand where sheep are the unquestioned masters of hill land, cattle are regarded as essential accessories because of their function as animated mowing machines.

A reduction of breeding cattle on hill and marginal land can often be compensated in financial terms by an improvement in the quality of the weaners. When farmers were greatly dependent on subsidies in the form of headage payments for both cows and their calves, the return on individual calves at point of sale was comparatively less important than it is today. The neat compact calf produced by a Blue Grey cow by an Aberdeen Angus bull is not the most desirable product, even though it produces very high-quality beef. The simple fact is that it has insufficient growth potential to appeal to the lowland fattener. When cows are bred solely for the production of fattening animals the expectation must be male animals that will weigh at least 500 kg at 15–16 months, not 350–400 kg. The need on most upland farms is for a milky cow with a reasonable frame, that is mated to a bull with a high growth potential. Increasingly, sires of the slaughter generation come from one or other of the continental breeds, notably the Charolais, Simmental or Limousin, that have made such an impact on British beef production over the past twenty-five years.

PLATE 1a

Cattle can be useful tools in maintaining good sheep grazing by controlling rough growth.

PLATE 1b

Cross Hereford cows grazing in semi-hill conditions.

ICI Photo.

PLATE 2a

Precision chop harvester in action. The silage is being treated with an additive contained in a 200 litre drum.

ICI Photo.

PLATE 2b

Eighteen-month beef cattle towards the end of their first summer at grass.

ICI Photo.

Chapter 3

LEYS OR PERMANENT PASTURE

'An abundance of fresh food is not compatible with a super-abundance of permanent grass.'

Sir George Stapledon made this statement at a time when pastures were neglected. He was expressing his profound belief in a system of farming where the plough was taken regularly round the farm to bring vigour to swards, based on selected species and varieties, rather than on volunteer plants of doubtful quality. The surveys that he and the late Dr William Davies had organised before the war revealed that an overwhelming proportion of the eight million hectares of permanent grass, existing at that time, consisted of bent grasses and had a grave deficiency of clover.

The translation of Stapledon's philosophies into farming practice was of enormous importance to Britain, especially during the war years. Some three million hectares of this poor pasture land, and large areas of rough grazings in addition, were brought under the plough, and most of it has been retained in alternate husbandry.

The whole process constituted a major revolution in British farming. It represented more than a regeneration of pastures. It brought about a revitalisation of the whole industry, in that it engendered a flexibility of outlook and a spirit of adventure that had been lacking since the days of high farming a century ago. When these events become history they will have a significance similar to those of the eighteenth century that led to the spread of the Norfolk four-course rotation.

THE CASE FOR LEY FARMING

One cannot argue against the validity of the ley farming concept under conditions of extreme pressure when food was rationed, for then it was virtually a question of food at any price. Nor can one suggest, under present conditions, a better system of land use for many of our farms which are above-average size in the main arable areas of Britain. Here ley farming is completely sensible, especially on the stronger soils where it is important to maintain good structure if crop yields are to be maintained.

In this context, one is thinking of those farms which are sufficiently large to carry the costs of mechanisation and which, as a group, are able to produce cereals and several break crops, such as sugar beet and potatoes, as efficiently as anywhere in the world. Cash crops are the first consideration on such farms and, in a sense, output from leys in the form of milk and meat is a by-product of tillage farming, for the primary function of the leys is to put heart into the land. Properly organised, the associated livestock enterprise can make an appreciable contribution to farm income, and the whole constitutes a well-integrated system of farming which has considerable resiliency in meeting the contingencies of seasons and prices.

The purpose and value of leys are very different, however, on farms where the principal income comes from grazing animals. Though this may seem like heresy, in that it cuts right across the Stapledon philosophy, the arguments in favour of very long duration pastures and good permanent grass, as opposed to short leys, are difficult to refute on a large number of our farms. This is especially true for farms of below-average size which are not suited to intensive cash cropping, and for farms of any size in the high-rainfall areas, especially on heavy soils where cropping is hazardous because of weather conditions at sowing and harvest.

Furthermore, the force of these arguments grows stronger

as our farming passes into an economic climate where the emphasis is less on volume of production than it is on economy of production. The basic reason for this statement is that the cheapest nutriment we can provide for stock is that from productive permanent pastures. Expressed in another way, a system of pastoral dairying, fat lamb production or cattle feeding, based on permanent grass, has a much lower potential cost structure than one that carries the cost of tillage implements and the expenses of renewing pastures every few years.

EXPERIMENTAL EVIDENCE

Protagonists of ley farming will immediately answer that it is impossible to get the level of output from permanent grass that one can get from leys, and so scale of operations will be reduced. Instead of milking 100 cows, or running 750 ewes, on a given area of grassland, a farmer will have to cut his carrying capacity to such an extent that any economies he will make by swinging to permanent grass will be more than accounted for by losses of income due to a scaling down of enterprises. After all, they will say, there is the evidence of those comparisons between leys and permanent grass initiated by the RASE and reported by William Davies and T. E. Williams. They concluded that if the permanent pastures of this country were replaced by well-managed leys there would be a 50 per cent increase in productivity.

There are two points which must be raised in answer to this. The first is that level of production is not synonymous with level of profit. The second is that a comparison is not valid if it is between well-managed leys and badly-managed permanent grass. The two types of grassland must have the same kind of management, and one would hope that it is an enlightened management which gives both types a chance to show their capacity.

It is important to note that in the RASE trials, where a comparison was made between a ley and a first-class permanent pasture in the Welland Valley, which is famed for the quality of its permanent grass, there was no difference in production from the two types of pasture. Where the comparisons were made between leys and poor permanent pasture, then a 50 per cent advantage could be attributed to leys. In our context we are not concerned with this kind of permanent pasture, but with the superior sorts that can be created by intelligent management.

A few years ago at Cockle Park there was a comparison between permanent grass and three different leys, based on perennial ryegrass and white clover. All four swards received identical grazing management and fertiliser treatments. At the end of three years the permanent grass showed a slightly higher output than the leys, and generally through the trial it had a much better performance during periods of drought. At any time during the growing season the permanent grass had more sheep-keep on it than any of the leys, and it had no establishment cost.

A long-term comparison has been made between permanent grass and leys on the Ministry of Agriculture Husbandry Farm in Lancashire, which is in a difficult farming area. It has revealed no advantage in using leys, and indeed results suggest that permanent grass may be the more economic proposition under these conditions of farming.

This comparison, almost more than any other, has made advisory officers stop short in their tracks and ask themselves whether their advocacies, based on an unquestioning acceptance of the Stapledon doctrine of ploughing and reseeding at regular intervals, are sound on farms where the purpose of grass is to feed stock rather than put heart into tillage land. Some of the more thoughtful have been debating whether they might not have been doing more good persuading farmers to improve their permanent grass by surface treatment rather than by ploughing, for there are still five million hectares of permanent grass in this country which have survived the war-time ploughing-up orders and the lure of subsidies that were offered for breaking old grass.

FLEXIBILITY OF LEYS

In any direct comparison of leys and permanent grass it must be said in favour of leys that they give much more flexibility in grassland management. Young leys, especially those that are based on early- and late-growing species, have a much longer growing season than permanent grass, which is generally regarded as a middle-of-the-season producer. This is certainly the case if the permanent pasture has a high proportion of bents or *Poa trivialis*, but if it is so managed that perennial ryegrass is the principal component, its spread of production does not differ markedly from an established perennial ryegrass ley.

In New Zealand, where the dairy industry is almost entirely based on permanent grass, a technique has been developed of over-sowing permanent pastures with an early-growing rye-grass. This has been remarkably successful in extending the availability of grazing without any need to plough.

Today with the availability of efficient forage harvesters and development of self-feeding or easy-feeding of silage, the pressure for out-of-season grass is not quite so great as it used to be. Sometimes one wonders whether we would not be more advantageously engaged growing more grass when conditions are favourable rather than complicating life in a struggle to grow out-of-season grass. By adopting such a policy, we could have vertical grazing at the silage face for five months of the year, and seven months' horizontal grazing on pasture for the remainder of the year. It would, of course, be essential to have one's silage making well organised, so that a first-class product is made from the grass that is surplus to immediate grazing needs.

Another argument in support of ploughing and reseeding is

a belief that a pasture is most prouductive in its first harvest year, and that there is a progressive deterioration from then onwards. The senior author was given a very different viewpoint as a young man in New Zealand, namely that it takes several years following establishment to get a pasture into full heart. The process, we were told, was one of applying phosphate, potash and lime, where these were necessary, to get a strong establishment of clover. Then, by heavy stocking, with a consequential heavy return of stock excrements, to get a mobilisation of fertility in the top few centimetres of the soil. This would support a vigorous growth of the high-producing species which would crowd out the unwanted volunteers that only gain ascendancy if fertility is depleted. There are millions of hectares of really productive permanent grass in New Zealand which provide support for this view.

Good management maintains the conditions that are essential for the dominance of sown species. If a ley deteriorates, one may be reasonably certain that some essential elements are lacking from the soil, or that there has been some form of mismanagement to tip the balance in favour of unwanted species.

In this last connection, one has to be a realist. Despite the best of intentions, the exigencies of farming may make it necessary to mismanage a pasture so that it deteriorates to a point where its restoration may be more quickly achieved by ploughing and reseeding than by any other means. Under such circumstances it may be sensible to plough, but this is a very different approach from a doctrinaire view that the plough should be put into a pasture every five or six years, whether it needs it or not. There is no need for every pasture on a farm to become a sacrifice area. Once a pasture has been established on a grassland farm every reasonable effort should be made to keep it in full vigour so that its establishment costs are spread over as many years as possible, even to the point where it can truly be described as permanent grass.

VIRTUES OF PERMANENT GRASS

Turning now to the intrinsic virtues of permanent grass, other than its cheapness, the first is its capacity to recover from poaching, which is far superior to that of a ley. This virtue is almost a handicap for permanent pastures, because most farmers, recognising this advantage, will punish an old pasture in the early spring. Many would be surprised at the greater productivity obtainable from their permanent grass if it was nursed as carefully as their leys and given the same fertiliser treatment.

A second virtue is its relative safeness so far as metabolic diseases and bloat are concerned. Old pasture, with its greater variety of species, is less incriminated in this connection than the simple quick-growing ley with grass all at the same stage of maturity.

A compensating disability is that a permanent pasture, under continuous stocking with the same species, may have a build-up of infections, for example, intestinal and lung worms. However there is no reason to believe that the clean-field technique (resting in alternate years from ewe and lamb grazing) is not just as effective with permanent pasture as it is with leys.

A further virtue of permanent grass is the way it stands up to summer drought, and its capacity to maintain milk yields in June and July, when leys are tending to run to head. At this time of the year permanent grass carries much more leaf than leys, and invariably when a herd moves from an established ley to good permanent grass, there is a lift in production.

IMPORTANCE OF A PERSPECTIVE

The issue between leys and permanent grass, however, is not a black and white one, for there are so many shades of grey, according to the conditions on individual farms. The wisest course for many farmers will be a combination of leys of varying duration with permanent grass. The leys will give that extra measure of flexibility in the provision of early grazing, so often missing if one has to rely on permanent grass alone.

The need for this flexibility will be greater on dairy farms than on lamb and beef producing farms, and this is fortunate, because dairying is better able to carry the higher costs of ley farming. At the same time, there is also a great deal to be said in favour of a high proportion of well-managed permanent grass on dairy farms not large enough to justify the high capitalisation involved in the ownership of a wide range of tillage implements.

One of the most serious criticisms one can make of the ley-farming doctrine is that it has encouraged the small man to make his farm a replica of the big farm, which is able to carry the cost of machinery and which has the elbow room to grow corn and provide bedding straw. Would it not be more profitable, in many instances, for someone with a 25 hectare farm to have all but, say, 4 hectares either in a well-managed permanet grass or very long leys? These 4 hectares could be devoted to a rotation of Italian ryegrass and late-sown kale, with 2 hectares of Italian being seeded down every spring. All straw, concentrated foods, and possibly even hay, could be bought in from someone able to produce these products more economically. Thus the only field equipment needed would be a tractor, a tipping trailer, a small forage harvester, a buck rake and a fertiliser spinner. Such cultivations as were needed for the small arable area could be done by contract.

A farm organised in this way would have a low investment in machinery and would be straighforward to run, for there are no complications and, with intensive management, it could have a milk output of at least 350,000 litres a year.

Such a plan of farming would, of course, demand a high level of management for permanent pasture. If you are happy to accept only what nature offers, which on all but the most fertile land will be daisies, buttercups and bents, then it is wise to forget all that has been said in favour of permanent pasture. If, on the other hand, you are prepared to provide the necessary fertility and management, you will find that the difference in production between leys and permanent pasture is surprisingly small, while cost of nutrients will be in favour of the permanent grass.

Chapter 4

MANAGEMENT AND PASTURE COMPOSITION

An association of pasture plants is never static, because the balance of the component species is constantly changing in response to a wide variety of stimuli. Some of these changes are progressive, for example, the steady deterioration that is so often observed in sown pastures due to an invasion of inferior species, as a result of mismanagement or failure to provide the necessary fertility to support the sown species. Conversely, though unfortunately less often one sees the reverse process, where a superior combination of species is created by appropriate management of poor pastures.

Other changes in pasture composition are seasonal in nature, for example, the greater dominance of grasses in the early spring and autumn, over clovers, which normally make their greatest contribution in the late spring and summer.

The aim of pasture management must be to maintain the most desirable combination of species by the various means which are under a farmer's control. This would be a relatively straightforward proposition if the appearance of the pasture were the only object, but a further overriding consideration is the basic needs of stock. Sometimes the requirements of animal and of pasture are in conflict, and there has to be sacrifice in one direction or the other to obtain the best economic result. Such decisions require very fine judgment, and herein lies the art of being a good grassland farmer.

There are very few definite rules that can be followed except that stock should not be made to suffer at critical times, for example, lactating cows or ewes, or young animals when they are making most active growth. Ewes and single-suckling cows, however, have low nutritional requirements when their offspring have been weaned, and can be made to work for their living in the interests of pasture management provided their body condition is fully restored at mating.

Similarly, there are critical stages in the life of pastures when they should not be abused. This is especially true in the early spring, when they are particularly vulnerable to poaching and to the ill effects of over-grazing; the younger a pasture is, the more liable it is to suffer from such maltreatment. This exemplifies one of the advantages of having some permanent pasture on a farm, because it has greater recuperative powers from poaching. In the absence of such land or, better still, housing to keep horned stock off pastures, it is preferable to work to a system of 'sacrifice fields' which are intended for immediate ploughing. In this way damage can be kept under control and the pastures which are intended to carry the burden of grazing or conservation in the subsequent year can be nursed in the early spring.

FACTORS DETERMINING COMPOSITION

When a pasture has been established there are three main sets of factors which determine pasture composition. They are:

(a) the physical condition of the soil
(b) soil fertility and fertiliser practices
(c) the timing and intensity of grazing and cutting.

There is a fourth factor which operates at the point of establishment, and this is the choice of seeds which are sown. The dice is loaded against the survival of sown species if non-persistent varieties are sown, for example commercial grades of so-called perennial ryegrass which have a high proportion of pseudo-perennial seed. Though this kind of seed is still on the market and is sometimes incorporated in seed mixtures, one of the great advances of the last thirty years has been the increased reliability of herbage seeds through the development of certification schemes.

Today there are abundant supplies of certified pasture seeds, either bred strains or genuine old pasture ecotypes, and though they cost slightly more per kilogram than commercial seeds, they are no more expensive ultimately because one can safely adopt lower seeding rates. The net result is that their virtues of persistency cost nothing. Anyone sowing only non-persistent commercial varieties in a pasture which is intended to have more than two years' duration should have his head examined, because he is being penny wise and pound foolish.

PHYSICAL CONDITIONS

Physical condition of a soil is only partly under the control of a farmer. He has to accept the inherent features of any given soil type, in so far as they are determined by such factors as aspect, and proportions of clay, silt, and sand. There are, however, two important farming operations which can have a considerable ameliorating effect on difficult soils. These are liming and drainage.

Lime has more than physical effects, because it corrects acidity and increases the availability of certain other plant foods. It has a profound effect on structure, and in this way improves soil moisture relationships. Lime is not expensive in Britain so there is no excuse for lack of lime being a limiting factor, except where considerations such as contour make its application prohibitively costly.

The benefits of drainage, in so far as pastures are concerned, are three-fold. The first arises from the fact that high-producing species will not persist under wet conditions, which favour an invasion of poorer grasses and useless weeds like rushes and buttercups. The second is an extension of the growing season, because wet land is also cold land. The third is that one has greater freedom in getting on to land to graze it, or for cultural operations like top-dressing or mowing. Though a farmer may not be able to face the cost of draining his whole

farm adequately at one fell swoop, he should at least have a
progressive programme of farm drainage to work to if surplus
soil water is a problem. Otherwise he cannot hope to realise the
potential of his grassland.

SOIL FERTILITY

The importance of providing adequate soil fertility, not only to
give the right environment for the persistence of desired
species, but to ensure that they are fully productive, should
require little stressing. Yet the unfortunate fact is that many
farmers are still much too parsimonious in their grassland
fertilising practices. On too many farms the decision to plough
a ley is made not because the land is needed for tillage but
because the ley has 'run out', even though management, apart
from fertilising, has been good.

Generally the principal deficiency is phosphate, and without
adequate phosphate clover will be sparse or virtually non-
existent. This was the great lesson of Somerville's classic work
at Cockle Park. A pasture without clover is only at half-cock,
unless one is prepared to use really massive dressings of
nitrogen. If there is not sufficient available nitrogen in the soil,
high-producing, nitrogen-demanding species like ryegrass will
disappear, to be succeeded by low-producing bents which can
tolerate nitrogen deficiency.

Potash is another vital plant food which is likely to be
deficient, not only on chalk soils and gravels which are
naturally poor in this respect, but even on heavier land which
has been used continuously for conservation purposes. Every
tonne of grass dry matter contains approximately the equivalent of 35 kg of muriate of potash, and unless remedial top-
dressing follows cutting, such land can quickly become potash
deficient. This is reflected in a loss of vigour in clovers, which in
cases of severe potash deficiency have characteristic brown
markings on the edge of their leaves.

Another element which is essential to clover growth is molybdenum, but is required only in very small quantities. Molybdenum deficiency has not been established on any scale in Britain, but there are parts of Australia and New Zealand where the application of as little as 150 gm of molybdenum salts per hectare makes all the difference in clover establishment.

Of the major elements, nitrogen has a profound effect on the balance of grasses and clovers in a sward. When land cropped with a long succession of exhaustive tillage crops, which have depleted soil nitrogen, is laid down to pasture, there is a very strong growth of clover in the first year. This especially is true on light soils like chalks and gravels, if there are adequate phosphate and potash reserves.

Gradually, however, the grass component achieves ascendancy as the nitrogen status of the soil is replenished by fixation of clovers, with the sub-surface transference of nitrogen being augmented by nitrogen returned in the excrements from grazing animals. This latter contribution can be a substantial one, amounting in one trial with only an average sort of pasture, to the equivalent of a tonne of sulphate of ammonia per hectare.

In a sense, clover is self destructive, for it encourages grass as it builds up the nitrogen status of soil to a point where there is a balance with these companion grasses. The nature of this balance will, of course, be greatly influenced by the management which is adopted. This, as later paragraphs will show, profoundly influences the proportion of clover in a sward.

The application of fertiliser nitrogen, as one would expect from the foregoing, has a considerable effect on the balance of clover in a sward. Even quite light dressings of, say, 50 kg N early in the season will reduce appreciably the proportion of clover in the sward during the subsequent summer. Heavy continued dressings of the order of 200 kg N per hectare annually will virtually eliminate clover if it is associated with ryegrass. The primary cause appears to be the stronger competitive power of grasses and the effects of smother. If the pasture is fairly tightly grazed the loss of clover is not so great as it is if the grass is allowed to get away. There may be a secondary effect with continued heavy dressings of some nitrogenous ferti-lisers, especially ammonium nitrate, of high soil acidity which must be contained by regular applications of lime.

It will be realised from this that there is something of a conflict between clover and fertiliser nitrogen. This is a point of great consequence in grassland farming, because there is a danger of falling between two stools. This will be debated at greater length in the next chapter, when an attempt will be made to resolve the issue as it affects different farming circumstances.

CUTTING AND GRAZING

Turning now to the effects of cutting and grazing management, the classic work in this field was that undertaken by Professor Martin Jones when he was at Jealott's Hill, some fifty years ago. Starting with a uniform pasture, he was able to create very diverse types by variations in timing and intensity of cutting and grazing. On the one hand, he created highly-productive ryegrass and white clover pastures, while on the other he allowed the processes of deterioration to move to the point where weeds and inferior grasses dominated.

This latter sward, which was the victim of over-grazing in the early spring and under-grazing in the summer, was typical of large areas of British grassland at that time. Unfortunately we have not yet seen the end of this sort of grassland, if the views provided by British Rail in the summer months can be taken as a fair indication of the state of our pasture management.

Martin Jones' work, and that of others who have developed our understanding of grassland ecology, have made it possible to state these fairly definite principles on which to base the handling of pastures:

(a) Hard grazing at a time when one species is making very active growth tends to put that species at a disadvantage relative to a companion species with a different growth rhythm. This is well illustrated by the usual management of grazing swards which are intended for the production of wild white clover, for example in Kent. Here ryegrass/white clover swards are hard grazed in the spring when the ryegrass is growing rapidly, but stock are removed in June when, in all but the wettest of seasons, the clover will achieve dominance. If the intention is to take ryegrass rather than clover seed, fields should be closed early in April following a top-dressing with nitrogen.

(b) Species vary in their response to light and shade, for example, the extreme pasture types of ryegrass and white clover require light if they are to compete successfully with a tall-growing, shade-enduring species like cocksfoot. Hard grazing of a Cockle Park mixture, especially with sheep, will soon result in what is virtually a pure ryegrass/white clover sward. Repeated annual cutting at an advanced stage of growth, or even continued lax grazing, will result in cocksfoot dominance and the almost complete disappearance of clover. Cocksfoot dominance becomes particularly marked if a sward is laid up for foggage for several years in succession. The same treatment encourages Yorkshire fog in permanent pastures.

(c) Mechanical damage, which is likely to occur on wet soils in the early spring, will open up a sward and promote conditions favouring the spread of light-demanding weeds like buttercups and daisies. We often see this result on heavy soils in several parts of England, for instance on the Weald of Kent and in the Midlands, and especially on small dairy farms, where stock going on the land when it is still wet do more harm to the pastures than good for themselves.

(d) The maintenance of vegetative growth in pasture plants is dependent on the pruning of tillers just before the point at which they throw up seed heads. Even an annual like wheat can be kept growing for several years, as Martin Jones has shown, if the seed-bearing shoots are cut before they break head. Once an annual has produced seed it will die.

PLATE 3a

Lime improves soil structure, corrects acidity and increases the availability of certain plant foods.

PLATE 3b

Applying nitrogen for an early bite. Timing of application of nitrogen dressings in spring is very important.

PLATE 4a
Good drainage encourages high-producing species, reduces weeds and extends the grazing season.

PLATE 4b
Welsh mountain draft ewes with Suffolk cross lambs at the Welsh Agricultural College's Tany-graig Farm. The intention should be to have lambs which are big enough in late April/May to make full use of the grass flush.

A perennial, though it survives after seeding, goes into a period of relative dormancy – a situation which is commonly shown by the poor aftermath growth in a pasture which is cut for hay at a very mature state.

(e) Continuous hard grazing in the growing season tends to reduce total production of a sward and to discourage the more productive species, except under the most favourable conditions of soil fertility. One must recognise in this connection that grass leaves have another function apart from that of providing grazing for livestock. They are also vital to the parent plant for their part in the photosynthetic process which creates the complex substances like carbohydrates and proteins that livestock utilise.

Woodman, working at Cambridge in the late twenties, illustrated this point very convincingly with simple mowing experiments where he cut pasture at intervals of one, two, three and four weeks. There was a progressive and substantial increase in yield as the intervals between cutting increased.

LEAF AREA AND ROOT DEVELOPMENT

Australian research workers have shown the importance of a pasture plant retaining a reasonable leaf area if one is to get sustained production. They argue that continuous grazing, provided there is no over-grazing and a reasonable leaf area is maintained, will give more production than rotational grazing or fold grazing, where a pasture is allowed to grow up and then is completely bared of leaf, especially if difficult environmental conditions follow. Undoubtedly this is true with fold grazing in the early spring if cold north-easterly conditions set in and the pasture is grazed right to the bone. Recovery will be very slow, though the ungrazed section of the field may still be making appreciable growth. Here it is possible that there is also a micro-climatic effect operating, for the grass cover could protect the ground against loss of heat.

In the early spring there is wisdom in adopting a policy of fairly lax rotational grazing of early-bite pastures, especially those containing clover, with the removal of stock from the field when there is leaf remaining to grow more leaf.

Another factor operating is the influence of defoliation on root development. Many years ago Jacques in New Zealand demonstrated the relationship of root development to top growth. Hard grazing reduces root development, and this may seriously impair production with the onset of dry weather unless the soil is fairly moist because of a high water table. Probably the latter factor is operating on Romney Marsh where, despite very close grazing, high production is achieved and a desirable pasture association preserved.

IMPORTANCE OF PASTURE CONTROL

It could be argued that some of the foregoing statements are conflicting, but one may fairly conclude that, for most conditions, it is wise to avoid over-grazing at those stages when pastures are making rapid vegetative growth. This may be achieved by lax continuous grazing or by controlled rotational grazing, without baring the pastures too hard so as to impair recovery.

The difficulty with lax continuous grazing is that the pasture tends to become a mosaic of short succulent growth which the stock prefer, and long mature growth which they neglect. Concentration of stock in large numbers for a short period gives more chance of preventing the mosaic developing and reducing the risk of weed invasion in the rough patches, but even here it may be necessary to use the mowing machine to prevent seed head emergence. The sensible thing to do, however, is not to mow for the sake of mowing but to integrate conservation with pasture control. Cutting grass for silage is more than a means of building up winter food reserves, for it is also a part of pasture management.

Later in the season, during July and August, it is often
essential to eat or cut a pasture very bare for its own good.
This point is reached when most grasses are undergoing their
summer pause and there is a good deal of neglected rough
growth which must be removed to prevent loss of clover. Here
a flock of ewes which have had their lambs removed are an ideal
tool to turn this rough growth into dung and urine. It will do the
ewes a lot of good too, if they are in high condition, because it is
in a farmer's interests to have them on short commons at this
time but not to the point where they are too lean at subsequent
tupping to achieve high ovulation rates.

From all this it will be realised that timing and intensity of
grazing can be varied to alter balance in mixed swards. For
instance, if clover is weak one must endeavour to prevent
shading in the spring, while cocksfoot dominance can be corrected by fairly close grazing throughout the year. A pasture is
a very malleable complex of species, both sown and volunteer,
but someone who has an understanding of the ecological
principles involved is in a position to control pasture
composition to suit his farming needs.

Chapter 5

THE IMPORTANCE OF CLOVER

Probably the greatest single step in the progress of British agriculture in the last three hundred years was the introduction of red clover. It made possible the much more productive system of farming which became known as the Norfolk four-course rotation. Tillage farmers learned very quickly the value of clover, not just as a forage but for enhancing the yields of succeeding crops.

White clover, the normal clover constituent of pasture, is not an introduced but an indigenous species, and no doubt it was an important component of grazing land on the more fertile soils in mediaeval times. Though it was included in sown pasture mixtures at least one hundred and fifty years ago, it was not until the beginning of this century that its essential value in pastures was realised.

Gilchrist working at Cockle Park, and Findlay at Aberdeen, were the two men, above all others, who brought home to farmers the importance of a vigorous white clover in the ley, not just for its contribution to production, but in stimulating growth in the following cereal crop. Today we associate the name of Stapledon with ley farming, but he always recognised the vital part that these two men played in establishing the system.

The value of clover in a sward was brought home to the senior author as a student in 1932 by a simple mowing experiment which compared the production of a pure ryegrass sward with one containing white clover. The latter was more than twice as productive, but analysis of the herbage showed that the difference was not accounted for by the clover fraction alone, because there was a 50 per cent greater yield of ryegrass where it was growing in association with clover. The stimulus came from the sub-surface transference of nitrogen which was fixed by bacteria in the clover-root nodules.

One New Zealand worker has put the nitrogen-fixing capacity of clover in a really good sward at a figure as high as 550 kg of applied N per hectare per annum. The figure for an equivalent pasture under British conditions, with lower soil temperatures and a much shorter growing season, will be only a fraction of this, but nevertheless it will be substantial, and probably not less than 170 kg N per hectare. The direct effect of clover nitrogen, of course, is augmented under grazing as opposed to mowing conditions. The animal retains only a small proportion of the nitrogen from its food, the balance being excreted in the dung and urine to make a further contribution to pasture growth.

The combined effect of sub-surface transference of nitrogen and excreted nitrogen was strikingly illustrated in an experiment which was conducted at Wye College a number of years ago. The trial constituted a comparison of the four white clovers – Dutch, New Zealand, S 100 and Kent. In the first year of the trial there was little to choose between the clovers, all swards producing approximately 800 kg liveweight increase per hectare from sheep. At the end of this year, however, there was a distinct tailing off in production from the Dutch paddocks, in which there was an almost complete loss of this short-lived variety. This was reflected in its performance in the second year, when liveweight production fell to just over 550 kg per hectare, while production from the other three clovers rose to the 900–1,000 kg level.

These relative positions were retained in the third year. In the fourth year there was also a loss in production from the New Zealand and S 100 clovers, which fell behind the Kent. These two rather upright growing types of clover did not, in a year of drought, stand up to the intensive grazing as did the prostrate Kent clover, which was evolved under conditions of very close grazing.

The effects of these clovers were reflected in a following potato crop which was used to measure residual fertility. The highest yields were obtained from the plots which had carried the Kent clover, and the lowest yields from the former Dutch plots.

Returning to the grazing phase of the trial, in the second and third years one would have thought that the companion S 23 ryegrass, common to all the swards, was a completely different variety on the Dutch paddocks from the ryegrass on the other three treatments. It was yellow, stemmy and, according to the behaviour of the sheep, very unpalatable. They spent approximately an hour longer each day grazing, and though lower stocking rates were imposed, there was no finish on the sheep. One could not have wished for a more graphic and convincing demonstration of the importance of sowing a reliable white clover and adopting methods of management which ensure its persistence.

LIMITATIONS OF CLOVER

It will be argued that no-one in his senses will ever sow a non-persistent white clover like Dutch in long leys. But this is beside the point, because for one reason or another there are millions of hectares of British grassland deficient in clover. As a consequence, they are incapable of producing to full capacity unless those concerned with their management are prepared to be heavy users of fertiliser nitrogen. We know from fertiliser usage surveys that this is not the case.

From a farm manager's viewpoint, clover nitrogen is cheap nitrogen. It costs no more than the price of the original seed and the lime, phosphate and potash, which form a basic dressing whether one uses fertiliser nitrogen or not. Though it is true that under British conditions one cannot hope to obtain the levels of herbage yields, even from a well-managed clovery pasture, that are obtained from pastures which receive really heavy nitrogen dressings, nevertheless the cheapest nutriment is obtained from a reliance on clover.

This brings us right into the business of grassland farming. Heavy nitrogen dressings are fully justified if (a) the cost of nitrogenous fertilisers is low relative to the returns for the animal products from grazing, and (b) if there is an efficient use of the additional herbage which is produced as the result of such dressings.

In New Zealand, where the sale value of milk or lamb is only about one-third of that in Britain and the cost of nitrogenous fertilisers is twice as high, it does not pay to apply nitrogen, even on the most efficiently managed dairy farms. Here economics dictate a reliance on clover nitrogen. It is, in fact, no very great hardship to do this. With the very long growing season, a farmer there can expect about double the dry-matter production we can expect in Britain when we rely on clover alone as a source of nitrogen.

FUNCTION OF FERTILISER NITROGEN

Our position constitutes a very different situation from that in New Zealand. If one reckons that a cow needs about 5,000 kg of grass dry matter annually in addition to concentrated food, about 0·8 hectares of good pasture without nitrogen will be required to support a milking cow. With heavy nitrogen dressings, of the order of 300–350 kg per hectare, it is reasonable to run a cow to less than half a hectare of grassland.

Expressed in another way, if a farmer carries 40 cow equivalents on 32 hectares of grassland without using nitrogen, an application of 350 kg N per hectare will enable him to push his herd up to 70–80 cow equivalents and in the process increase his gross income by at least two-thirds. There will, of course, be a proportionate increase in variable costs such as those for purchased food, veterinary services and so on, but fixed costs such as those of management and rent will be spread over the much larger output. If work can be organised through a better layout and appropriate mechanisation, there need be no increase in labour costs, but there can be a very substantial increase in net income. This has been demonstrated by many successful dairy farmers.

Heavy nitrogen use in this way has a special appeal to the small dairy farmer, who is particularly handicapped by lack of land and under-use of available labour. It is within his power to add the equivalent of at least 50 per cent to the area of his grassland, and though this will involve a considerable outlay per hectare, he is able to increase net income because of the considerable economies of scale which can be effected.

Nowhere is this philosophy of grassland dairy farming seen to better effect than in the Netherlands, where the contribution of clover is virtually ignored because it does not permit the intensity of farming which is necessary for a livelihood on these small Dutch farms. While the cost of grass nutrients is higher than it would be if they relied on clovery pastures, nevertheless it is still considerably lower than it is for purchased foods, and there are the compensating economies from being able to keep more cows on a farm.

The Dutch example is being followed in the United Kingdom, especially in Northern Ireland, another country of small farms, which fortunately has the sort of climate that assures full value from applied nitrogen. However, many of our dairy farmers who are attempting to make good use of their grass tend, in a typically British fashion, to steer a middle course between the Dutch and New Zealand extremes. There can be a danger of falling between two stools by such an action, because of a conflict that exists between clover and bag nitrogen at low rates of application. For instance, if one applies 70 kg N per hectare in the early spring, there is an immediate encouragement of grass at the expense of clover. If no further nitrogen is applied, there is usually an appreciable slumping of subsequent production due to the impairment of clover contribution. The net result is that total annual production will be no more, and sometimes less, than it would have been if nitrogen had not been applied. The main advantage that this nitrogen gives is a better spread of grass production.

It can be a very sensible management decision to forgo some May grass in order to cut down cake feeding in late March and early April, but it is questionable if the application of this sort of early dressing to the whole of the grassland on a farm is the right course. If one is steering a middle course and trying to get the best of both worlds, it may be better to be a Dutchman on an appropriate part of the farm and a New Zealander on the rest of the farm. One would apply the heavy nitrogen dressings to pastures such as those based on Italian ryegrass, which are particularly responsive to nitrogen, or old leys which are probably due for the plough because they have lost their clover content.

The above comments apply particularly to swards which are intended for grazing rather than cutting, and they are also more applicable to areas with a good summer rainfall and therefore more likely to have a stronger clover contribution. The case for using higher nitrogen applications is stronger in the more difficult grassland areas, in the north of the country, and on heavy soils. The occasional nitrogen dressing appears to be used more efficiently by a pasture that is allowed to grow to the cutting stage than one that is closely grazed.

Any advocacy of a heavy use of nitrogen must be qualified with the stipulation that, to make it pay, one must adopt really efficient methods of utilisation. It is not enough to grow 50 per cent more herbage by applying a given quantity of nitrogen over the course of the year. It must be turned into 50 per cent more milk or meat.

If there are surpluses beyond immediate grazing needs, these must be turned into hay or silage reserves so that any subsequent increase in carrying capacity can be made with confidence. If any efforts to increase the intensity of grassland farming by a greater use of nitrogen are to be successful, there will be a concomitant of more intensive stocking, and the conservation of surpluses in such a way that a first-class product results.

There may be some latitute for being a little casual with grass dry matter that costs £30 per tonne, but if it costs £50 per tonne then it must be efficiently utilised. It is not enough either, that one's grassland management is good. Whole farm management must also be of a matching quality when one moves into high farming.

ECONOMICS OF NITROGEN USE

This emphasis on efficiency draws a sharp line between the economics of nitrogen use on dairy farms as opposed to fat lamb and cattle feeding farms. The very much lower efficiency of meat as opposed to milk production does not make it generally possible to follow a high-nitrogen policy on meat producing farms. A 50 per cent increase in grass production will not, in the first place, be matched by anything like a 50 per cent increase in gross income. In the second place, the limited margins one has to work with necessitate very cheap food, if a reasonable profit is to be made. This means, in effect, an acceptance of a lower rate of stocking as a consequence of relying mainly on clover nitrogen.

This does not mean that there is no place for nitrogen top-dressings on the grassland of the sheep and cattle farmer. Its use is justified on grass crops intended for conservation or for some early bite, when this will replace more expensive alternative foods, and for the production of foggage where this is used in the back-end as a substitute for a more expensive forage crop. The use of nitrogen will, however, be much more opportunist than it will be on the intensively stocked dairy farm.

There is a place for heavy nitrogen applications, of the order of 250 kg per hectare, in the 18-month system of beef production based on autumn-born dairy-bred calves. In their first and only summer they are grazed intensively not with the objective of maximising liveweight gain per animal as much as liveweight gain per hectare. Subsequently when they move into winter quarters for the second time the aim is to bring them quickly to slaughter condition on a diet of quality silage supplemented with barley. Under these circumstances the efficient farmer is fully justified with such a level of nitrogen use.

It is stressed that if one is going to rely on clover nitrogen, a very real effort must be made to encourage a vigorous growth of clover in the sward by using all the management devices at a farmer's disposal. We have been thinking in terms of a pasture which will produce 6,000 kg of leafy dry matter without the aid of fertiliser nitrogen, but this is substantially in advance of the yield of the average pasture. The average pasture, however, has insufficient clover because of failure to provide adequate lime, phosphate and potash, because it has been taken too frequently to an over-mature stage before cutting, or because it has not been properly grazed.

The famous fattening pastures of this country invariably have a good balance of grass and clover, because these are on land of high natural fertility and they are always scrupulously managed. Good grazing management can be applied to any pasture, and if the soil is deficient in some essential plant food it is no great problem to make this deficiency good. As the late Dr William Davies said on many occasions, referring to grass on lowland farms, there is very little poor land in Britain, but a lot of poor grassland management. Fortunately this situation is changing rapidly as land becomes more expensive and there are other economic pressures operating to encourage a better appreciation of the importance of well-managed grass in improving the viability of livestock farms.

Chapter 6

PASTURE PRODUCTIVITY

There are two main aspects to productivity, namely the total quantity of dry matter that a pasture produces, and the quality of that dry matter in terms of digestible nutrients. In addition, the herbage must be palatable, and it must be safe in the sense that it does not impair the health of stock or, in the case of dairy cows, produce milk taints.

We do not yet know enough about certain health aspects, and for some farmers the fear of bloat or grass tetany is still a deterrent against intensive grassland farming. Fortunately, trouble of this nature is not continuous and widespread, but every now and then some farmers run into real trouble. However, one can be reasonably hopeful of an early breakthrough on these problems, with the steady advances that are now being made in rumen physiology.

FEEDING VALUE OF GRASS

Broadly the same factors which influence yield also affect quality, namely botanical composition, soil fertility levels, and management, with this last factor having an overriding influence on the other two. It is not enough to establish desirable species on a well-fertilised soil. One must always offer herbage which is at a stage of growth where it will do stock most good, and this calls for an understanding of the con siderable chemical changes that take place in pasture plants from the first stage of active spring growth through to full maturity.

The work of Woodman at Cambridge and Fagan at Aberystwyth, more than fifty years ago, defined these changes and related them to changes in feeding value. As pasture matures, there is a progressive fall in its protein content, which is accompanied by an increase in fibre. There is an accompanying fall in digestibility, though digestibility is remarkably well maintained up to the point of seed head emergence, when a rapid deterioration takes place.

The dry-matter content of herbage that is still in the vegetative phase of growth has all the attributes of a concentrate. It is extremely digestible, and it is rich in protein, often to the point of being in excess of the animal's needs. However, it is cheap protein, and so one need not be concerned that good pasture is slightly unbalanced in this sense. The very high quality of grass dry matter at this stage prompted Woodman to advocate the artificial drying of grass to provide a concentrate which would compete with protein-rich feeds such as linseed or soya-bean meals.

At ear emergence, pasture still retains a considerable amount of leaf and its digestibility is reasonably high. After flowering and the maturing of seed, it quickly moves to a stage where it is little better than straw. Not only is the protein content low, it also has a very poor digestibility because the soluble or easily-digested carbohydrates like sugars and starches have been converted to fibre, with its low-energy availability to the animal. Intake of dry matter is also impaired by this lower digestibility because of the slower passage of food through the alimentary tract.

Work at the Hannah Dairy Research Institute and elsewhere has shown that the deterioration in feeding value in pasture as it ages is due to more than reduced digestibility. Mature herbage, such as hay or silage that has been cut after the flowering stage, gives rise to a very different sort of rumen fermentation from that resulting from eating young herbage. With young herbage the fermentation is very similar to that which occurs with concentrated foods. The end-products have a very high efficiency for production purposes, whereas the end-products of digestion of mature herbage, though they are valuable in satisfying maintenance requirements, are very inefficient for production purposes.

If a farmer is able to offer his cows only hay or silage made from very mature herbage, then it is necessary, if he is going to obtain a reasonable level of production, to feed concentrates at a heavy rate. If, on the other hand, he is able to provide well-made silage, cut at the flag stage, and hay that has been cut at the early flowering stage, he will be providing bulk foods with a concentrate-sparing function, because the products of their digestion have much the same attributes as the products of concentrate digestion.

With a knowledge of these facts, it is now possible to define two primary objectives for a grassland farmer. The first is a provision of a succession of leafy herbage over the grazing season. The second is the conservation of surpluses over and above immediate grazing requirements at a stage of growth that will give them, in the form of hay and silage, a production as well as a maintenance function.

Fortunately, the two objectives are fully compatible, and their attainment will secure the maximum production of nutrients over the year. The aim is to use the grazing animal and the mowing machine to keep pastures juvenile and in active growth. If one delays cutting until an advanced state of maturity, aftermath growth will be slow, because young tillers will have been smothered and there will be a time lag before fresh tillers take their place. One should try to avoid leaving cutting to the point where there is a yellow bottom to the sward. The aim should be to retain some greenness, for this will ensure a quicker recovery. Herein lies one of the great advantages of ensilage over haymaking in this doubtful climate of ours.

Though, in theory, it is right to cut grass for hay when it is still full of nutriment, unfortunately at this stage it is also full of sap and is inclined to pan down in the swathe. This in turn slows the rate of drying. On balance, it is much easier to make good silage than good hay earlier in the season, but at the same time it pays to be an opportunist. If, as so often happens, good haymaking weather comes in late May, it is sensible to turn from silage to haymaking, provided one has equipment that will fluff up the cut grass and speed the drying process.

In this context, however, the type of conservation product is irrelevant. The important issue is a succession of fresh aftermaths being made available for grazing as the season advances. The man who leaves his mowing until July will have a large area of poor aftermath coming in at the one time, and he has lost much of the benefit of using the mowing machine as a tool in pasture management.

This last point is of great consequence where one is using intensive methods of grazing, such as folding behind an electric fence or rotational grazing, with subdivision into small paddocks. After the second grazing, a considerable proportion of the pasture will be fouled by excrements and will be neglected by the stock. No amount of grassland harrowing will correct this. The best approach is to endeavour to alternate mowing with grazing, so that one combines the operation of building up winter reserves with the maintenance of a leafy succession of clean growth which will be attractive to stock.

BOTANICAL COMPOSITION

Turning now to the influence of botanical composition, there appears to be surprisingly little difference in feeding value of the more common pasture species, at corresponding stages of growth. The main feature which determines whether a species is good or bad is duration of leafy growth. A grass like common bent is late in starting spring growth, it moves fairly quickly to the reproductive stage, and it has a limited capacity for autumn growth. A pasture-type of ryegrass, on the other hand, has a much longer growing season, and with comparable management has a much more favourable leaf–stem ratio, as well as a much greater productivity.

PLATE 5a

Phosphate deficiency leads to lack of clover in the sward. Grass on right had received no phosphate since sown three years before, while that on left received phosphate at the end of the third year and shows marked clover growth.

PLATE 5b

Professor Martin Jones transformed uniform pastures into diverse types by variations in timing and intensity of grazing and cutting.

PLATE 6

Mechanical damage is most likely to occur on wet soils. It opens the sward and promotes conditions favouring the spread of light-demanding weeds such as buttercups and daisies.

At the same time, it must be stressed that good management can make a considerable difference to the value of what are generally considered to be inferior grasses. For instance, on peat soils in New Zealand extremely high production is obtained from pastures which contain a large proportion of Yorkshire fog. Leafiness is maintained by intensive grazing for short periods, which are followed by longer periods of rest.

We have, unfortunately, little reliable information on the relative feeding values of the main grass species, let alone differences between varieties within species. Some work at the Hannah a number of years ago indicated a much lower dry matter intake by cows grazing cocksfoot as compared with perennial ryegrass. Digestibility studies on S 37 cocksfoot and S 23 and S 24 perennial ryegrass at the Grassland Research Station, Hurley, have shown cocksfoot to be at a considerable disadvantage as compared with the ryegrasses, at all stages of growth. Even in April, when over 80 per cent of the herbage consisted of leaf, the digestibility of the cocksfoot was only 70 per cent, as compared with 75 per cent for the S 24. This difference persisted through to the fully-mature stage in June, when there was virtually no growth. Similar differences were maintained in the digestibilities of the monthly regrowth. Both ryegrasses maintained digestibilities in the 70–75 per cent range from June to October, but the cocksfoot figure was never better than 70 per cent, and fell to as low as 60 per cent in October.

After seeing these results, and the suggestion from the Hannah work that cocksfoot is less palatable than ryegrass, it is not surprising that so many intensive grassland farmers have such a poor opinion of cocksfoot for production purposes. Cocksfoot appears to be a better friend of the cake merchant than it is of a farmer who is trying to obtain the maximum amount of milk from grass. That certainly is our impression, from experiences with cocksfoot in both the south and the north of England.

Though Hurley work shows that the digestibility of S 23 is maintained until well into June, when ear emergence takes place some three weeks later than S 24 ryegrass, it is unfortunately much too late in starting growth in the spring. Its palatability is in some doubt as well. In our experience it does not seem so attractive to sheep and cattle as some of the Continental pasture strains of ryegrass, such as *Melle*. It is not enough to have grasses which have good digestibility values. They must also be attractive to the stock that graze them. Unquestionably, much of the value of the timothy/meadow fescue ley for milk production is attributable to its palatability, and the same is true of Italian ryegrass.

FACTORS AFFECTING PALATABILITY

Species or variety alone does not determine palatability, which is also influenced by stage of growth as well as freedom from any form of fouling. Any quick-growing leafy pasture which is free from objectionable plants like stinking mayweed will invariably have a high degree of palatability. So those conditions which promote active growth, such as adequate moisture and soil fertility, also promote palatability. Palatability with its effect on intake is probably one of the main reasons why a direct reseed in its maiden year has such a capacity to stimulate milk yields.

Variety in a sward also seems to contribute to its palatability. At Wye College a realignment of fencing resulted in the inclusion of a small area of cocksfoot in a mainly ryegrass field, and a small area of ryegrass in the adjacent field sown to cocksfoot. It was remarkable that the hardest grazed parts of both fields were these two small transfer portions.

The habit of stock foraging along hedgerows probably arises from their liking for variety, though some people attribute this to a craving for something that highly improved pastures lack. Probably this assumption goes too far. One cannot, for instance, conclude that because cows which break into a garden seem to have a penchant for one's most precious plants, that these should be included in pasture seed mixtures.

MINERAL DEFICIENCIES

There is, however, a school of thought that believes that mineral-efficient herbs such as burnet, plantain, chicory and yarrow should be included in ley mixtures or should be sown in strips down the field to minimise the alleged dangers of too much purity. The literature, however, is conspicuously short of convincing arguments on the wisdom of including these herbs, apart from the fact that they are generally richer than grass in such minerals as calcium and magnesium. White clover also shares this quality of being richer in these minerals than grasses, and it has the additional advantage that it will fix atmospheric nitrogen.

A trial at Cockle Park, which compared a clover dominant sward with a normal ryegrass/white clover sward, both with and without sown herbs, did not reveal any advantage from the inclusion of herbs, as measured by the thrift of grazing ewes and lambs. If anything came out of the early stages of the trial, it was the advantage of having a high proportion of clover in the sward, for in the first year the best lambs came off the very clovery swards.

Generally speaking, there is little to worry about in respect of mineral content of swards which have a good balance of grass and clover and are well fertilised. There are, however, exceptions to this rule, and the most notable relate to those areas which are known to have a deficiency of copper or cobalt. Pasture improvement on such areas seems to aggravate these trace element deficiencies, for the greater growth of herbage dilutes even further the small quantities of available cobalt and copper.

Perhaps the most spectacular example of cobalt deficiency

was that of thousands of hectares of so-called 'bush-sick' country in New Zealand, where cattle and sheep would waste away on what appeared to be first class pastures. Then it was established that the difference between death and normal health on these pastures was a matter of a few parts of cobalt per million parts of dry matter. Normal rates of top-dressing with superphosphate, with cobalt salts added at the rate of a kilogram per tonne of superphosphate, amply safeguarded the pastures. A similar correction of copper deficiency has been achieved by the application of 'copperised' superphosphate.

We have areas in Britain which are either copper or cobalt deficient, but these are fairly well defined, and symptoms of deficiency are quickly recognised by veterinarians. One of the most likely areas for a copper deficiency is on reclaimed peat – in fact, in some parts of the world, copper deficiency disease is described as 'peat scours'. Prevention may be effected by drenching or by the provision of mineral licks, but the most convenient and certain method, if deficiencies are known, is to incorporate the missing element in a fertiliser which is regularly applied to the pasture.

GRASS TETANY

One of the most intriguing, and one of the most serious, problems of mineral deficiency associated with the grazing animal is grass tetany, or hypomagnesaemia. A condition of the disease is the very low level of magnesium in the blood. Because of this, it can be loosely classed as a deficiency disease, but not in the same category as cobalt deficiency.

The disease is generally associated with two distinct periods – one in the winter prior to active pasture growth, and the other during the spring when growth is active. There is also a liability of the disease occurring during the autumn, again when grass is making fairly rapid growth. It is scarcely correct to call the disease grass tetany in the late winter when the intake of grass is very low. Then it is probable that the occurrence of the disease is due to a very low intake of magnesium, because of the nature of the diet, and the action of certain stresses such as those caused by the demands of lactation or difficult weather conditions. The other period of grass tetany, namely that during the period of active pasture growth, is of more concern to progressive grassland farmers.

Knowledge of the disease and the conditions that are associated with it is at that annoying stage where nobody can be categoric about it, certainly not to the point of laying down definite instructions for the complete avoidance of trouble. Young, quickly-growing pasture appears to be particularly suspect, and in the view of some farmers this implicates nitrogenous fertilising. Whether this is a correct suspicion or not has not been satisfactorily established. Though the disease occurs in many herds which are grazing early-bite pastures which have received nitrogen, there are also many herds on the same sort of grazing which are free of the trouble. It is certainly not a black and white issue.

Work in Eire and the Netherlands has incriminated high nitrogen usage when this is associated with heavy dressings of potash. This boils down to the same thing as heavy dressings of nitrogen on soils with large reserves of potash, which may have been created by heavy stocking and the return of urine over a period of years – a condition that is likely to be found in home paddocks.

The biochemistry of the situation is not yet fully understood, but it is known that if there is a high availability of potash during a period of active growth, there is a luxury uptake of this element at the expense of magnesium. This is especially true of grasses as opposed to clovers, and it is grass rather than clover that makes the main contribution to grazing in the early spring when nitrogen has been used to stimulate growth. No-one can say for certain, however, that a low magnesium content of this early spring growth is the direct cause of grass tetany. There may be other factors operating, for example upsets in the animal's normal physiological processes which impair its capacity to mobilise the considerable reserves of magnesium it carries in its body.

Whatever the ultimate explanation, the fact remains that the onset of the disease can be really terrifying. In the spring of 1952, at Wye College farm, we were tremendously proud of the fact that our 60-cow Ayrshire herd was completely supported by grass in April and was producing 1,000 litres per day. This was a very satisfactory level, in view of the fact that the herd consisted mainly of autumn calvers and included a higher than normal proportion of heifers.

Then we struck trouble. Four high-producing cows died suddenly, two of them within minutes of having given their usual amount of milk, and nearly half the herd developed a 'jittery' condition which one associates with maltreatment. The veterinarian who attended the herd had no difficulty in diagnosing the trouble, because it was a copy-book case of hypomagnesaemia. Affected cows were injected and the herd was moved immediately from the quick-growing ley on which they had been grazing to an old permanent pasture. In addition they were given a small ration of concentrates fortified with calcined magnesite, so that each cow got at least 55 grams of this mineral per day. The condition disappeared almost as quickly as it arrived, though the herd did not return to its previous level of production.

Which of the remedial actions was the most efficacious no-one can say, but the whole incident left one indelible impression, namely the importance of making gradual changes in the feeding of livestock. One cannot hear a farmer say that he has suddenly dropped supplementary feeding in the early spring because he has ample grass without giving him the warning of this experience. This does not mean that we no longer advocate the provision of early bite through the growing of a species like Italian ryegrass, which receives a heavy dressing of nitrogen. To advise another course would be as rational as an advocacy of a return to the horse and cart to cut down the incidence of road accidents. The tempo of our farming is such that we have to use such aids to lower the cost of milk production, but there are certain limits to be observed until such time as we have a better understanding of the complexities of ruminant nutrition.

Until we are in a position to produce really safe early bite, it is wise to continue to feed some additional food which has been fortified with calcined magnesite until the grass has 'hardened', as it does in May. Significantly, the safe period for grass coincides with the time when clover starts to make an appreciable contribution to grazing.

Clover, however, is not only possessed of virtues, for dominantly-clover swards are seriously implicated with the occurrence of bloat or hoven. Fortunately, in Britain, bloat is not the nightmare it is in certain parts of New Zealand, and under our conditions of management it can hardly be described as a really serious hazard over the general run of farms.

AUTUMN GRASS

Any account of pasture quality is incomplete without some discussion of differences between spring and autumn pasture. Chemically these are small, though sugar levels may be slightly higher in spring pasture, and yet there is a considerable difference in feeding value in favour of spring pasture. Probably the main reason for the difference in quality is the rather higher moisture content of autumn pasture, which is aggravated by the presence of a considerable amount of free moisture as the result of heavy dews. Comparison between dried grass from the two seasons, cut at corresponding stages of growth, reveal practically no difference in feed value.

Under grazing conditions there are probably other contributory reasons. There is a greater liability of autumn grass being fouled and, in consequence, having a lower palatability. There are also greater risks from such infections as husk or intestinal worms, which appear to be more potent in their effects in the autumn than they are earlier in the season.

There is, of course, little that the farmer can do to improve the quality of autumn grass to the point where it is comparable with spring grass. He has to accept its relative inferiority and make allowance for this in his supplementary feeding plans, especially when he is dealing with freshly-calved cows – a point which will be discussed in greater detail at a later juncture. At the same time it has to be stressed that autumn grass is still capable of making a most valuable contribution to the feeding of a herd or flock.

It is well worthwhile to make a special effort to build up reserves of back-end grazing and to ration them so that they are not wasted. When the last of the autumn good grass is finished, even though it may be as late as December, one invariably sees this reflected by a drop in milk yields, despite efforts to make compensating changes by the provision of other food. It may well be that autumn grass is equally valuable to some farmers as early bite, but this is a point we will argue about later in the book.

Chapter 7

PASTURE UTILISATION

Efficient use of pastures depends on seven principal factors:
1. Inherent productivity of the livestock that it carries;
2. Quality of management of this stock;
3. Health status;
4. System of grazing that is adopted;
5. Efficiency of conservation practices;
6. Levels of feeding supplementary to pasture;
7. Intensity of stocking.

The first three factors are outside the scope of this book except insofar as health considerations and general thrift are affected by management decisions. For instance, in the rearing of young stock – be they calves or lambs – worm burdens can be materially reduced by appropriate resting of pasture to break the cycle of infection. Again, both fertiliser practices and the feeding of supplements in the spring can affect the level of incidence of hypomagnesaemia. These are matters of great concern to a farmer who is trying to get the best out of his grass.

We shall be dealing with two further factors, supplementary feeding and conservation practices, later in this book but they are mentioned here principally to stress the fact that none of these factors can be considered in isolation from the rest as they interact together. The economic utilisation of grassland is complex where the successful farmer combines his skill of stockmanship with sound management decisions relating to the handling of both stock and pastures.

The remaining two factors, intensity of stocking and system of grazing, are very closely linked. It can generally be accepted that the higher the intensity of stocking, the more important it is to have controlled grazing, whether this is achieved by folding, using an electric fence or more permanent subdivisions to permit some form of paddock grazing. The more stock one has on a farm, the more important it becomes to have a planned system of pasture production and a means of rationing the available grazing to minimise wastage in its various forms.

GRAZING MANAGEMENT SYSTEMS

We can distinguish these forms of grazing management:
(1) Set stocking where a herd or a flock remains on the same field over a long period, sometimes for the greater part of the grazing season.
(2) Rotational or paddock grazing where there is close subdivision and stock are concentrated in one enclosure for short periods before being moved to a fresh enclosure.
(3) Fold grazing where stock are given a ration of grass, usually at least once daily behind an electrified wire which can be quickly moved to its next position.

There are variants of these systems. Rotational grazing can be integrated with conservation on the same area or, in dairy farming, a two-sward system can be practised using one area which is principally used for conservation. Later we will be discussing the pros and cons of these different approaches. Another variant of rotational grazing is that developed for intensive fat lamb production, known as forward creep grazing, where suckling lambs have preferential access over their mothers to the next paddock in the rotation.

Set stocking is generally characteristic of less intensive forms of utilisation, e.g. the grass fattening of bullocks where equation of appetite and availability of nutrients is achieved by adjustments of stock numbers. It is generally recognised that store cattle finish more quickly if they are subjected to the minimum of disturbance and this is usually the situation with set stocking. The same applies in fat lamb production but inevitably, though individual performance is better, there is a loss of production per unit area because it is not possible to maintain a really high intensity of stocking.

Stocking intensity is unquestionably one of the key factors in determining relative efficiency of pasture utilisation. It can be taken as axiomatic that maximum production per hectare is not coincident with maximum output per individual. In other words, in order to effect the highest level of conversion of grass nutrients into milk or meat or wool, there must be some sacrifice of individual performance, but this must never proceed to the point where net returns are impaired. The intensive grassland farmer has to walk a tight-rope in this connection, and especially is this true in dairying, but fortunately there are aids in the form of supplementary feeding to help him in his balancing act.

ROTATIONAL GRAZING

Almost the best approach to an understanding of this problem comes from an examination of the advances that have been made in intensifying pasture production that have occurred over the past sixty years. A key issue in this has been the development of rotational grazing.

Sir Bruce Levy, possibly the world's greatest authority on grass farming at that time, when addressing the Farmers Club in 1949 stated that intensive rotational grazing gave 50 per cent more production than uncontrolled stocking of grassland. His statement was not questioned by those present, though he had little direct experimental evidence to support it. His views were based on many years of experience over a critical period in the development of grassland farming in New Zealand. As a young man, he saw the pioneering phase of the industry, when farmers were grazing their stock extensively amid blackened stumps on pastures that depended largely on residual fertility of the bush burns. But by the time he made this statement New Zealand had achieved the status of being one of the foremost grassland countries.

In the interim, the German development of the Hohenheim system of intensive rotational grazing, and Woodman's work on intervals of cutting and its influence on productivity, had a tremendous impact on New Zealand grassland practice, especially on dairy farms. The pattern of development was one of closer subdivision of farms so that there were as many as twenty paddocks, each of which was grazed in turn over a period of 1–5 days, according to season, first by the milking herd and then by followers, and then rested for a period of 2–3 weeks. The aim was to graze at the leafy 100–150 mm stage, and to conserve the spring surplus of silage or hay by dropping a proportion of the paddocks from the grazing rotation.

It was a beautifully simple system to advocate and it was, moreover, highly successful. Top farmers on the better land were carrying a dairy cow and her share of replacement stock, and producing 7,000 litres of Jersey milk on half a hectare of grassland without the aid of supplementary crops or concentrates. The plough, in fact, became a rarity on these farms, and the whole of the feeding was based on permanent grass.

There were many other factors other than the system of grazing contributing to this spectacular improvement, for example, the effects of herd recording, the improvement of stock, better management and control of disease, and a greater use of phosphatic fertilisers. But undoubtedly the system of grazing played a substantial part.

However, it is highly doubtful whether the direct effects of quick grazing followed by rest were as great as Woodman's findings would have led one to expect in determining this improvement. Cutting with a mowing machine, especially when the sward is bared very closely (as it is with the lawn mower commonly used in small experiments), is a very different matter from defoliation by grazing, especially when the animals concerned are cattle. Not only is there more leaf left to effect recovery, but the pasture under continuous grazing tends to assume a more prostrate form, which, though short, can be remarkably leafy – a condition seen clearly on farms adopting intensive set stocking with sheep. In addition, the mowing machine does not return excrements, with their stimulating effects on growth.

Weight is added to this view by results obtained by Australian workers who have established, under their conditions, that continuous grazing, provided it retains a reasonable leaf area, does not suffer in comparison with rotational grazing in respect of nutrients produced from a pasture. There is also confirmatory evidence from a long-term New Zealand trial at Ruakura with dairy cattle, which will be referred to in more detail later, that there is no appreciable difference in dry matter production from pastures subjected to either continuous or controlled rotational grazing, provided there is full utilisation without over-grazing.

PLANNING OF FOOD SUPPLIES

Undoubtedly the main advantage of controlled grazing is derived from two principal features of the system. The first is what one may call a rationalisation of the farming programme to ensure a continuous supply of good food over a long grazing season, with the opportunity of conserving surplus grass for those periods when growth is inadequate for the needs of the herd. The second is the confidence that such a system gives one to increase the intensity of stocking, which, in our opinion, is by far the most important single factor in determining degree of pasture utilisation.

These points can be clarified by a consideration of a situation where a herd or flock is continuously grazing one large field from early spring to late autumn. At the point of commencement of growth there will be inadequate feed, and each blade of grass will be pruned as it comes within grazing range. Of necessity, the stock have to receive supplementary feed to keep up production.

By mid-spring, there is an equation of stock appetite and grass growth. But within a matter of a few weeks, as grass gets ahead of stock, the field is a mosaic of closely-grazed and neglected patches, with the latter running up to head to deteriorate in quality. There is a surplus in the field, but it is not practicable to cut it for silage, and the best one can do is to top it, or leave it to provide a bit of rough grazing if there is a summer drought. In this event it will have a limited value in maintaining stock, but no worthwhile productive function.

More often than not, it will remain till late autumn, when it may not be cleared by grazing. In the meantime, it will have affected sward composition, as less desirable grasses for production, like Yorkshire fog, *Poa trivialis*, and cocksfoot, will have achieved dominance in these rough patches and clover will have been suppressed. Too often these rough patches are carried over into the spring, aggravating the situation and accelerating the process of sward deterioration.

Contrast the management of that field with a subdivision either by permanent or temporary fencing. Each area can be grazed in turn, taking precautions to avoid over-grazing, until there is a surplus of grass. Then a proportion of the paddocks can be withdrawn from the grazing rotation for mowing. As these come back into grazing with clean fresh aftermaths, paddocks which have been grazed twice can, in their turn, be closed for conservation and cleaning, which is achieved by the one act of cutting. The summer period of reduced growth brings every paddock back into the rotation.

At this time of the year there are often some animals that do not require a high plane of nutrition and these can advantageously be used in a tight system of grazing to turn rough feed into dung and urine, and, thereby, mobilise fertility to promote fresh growth and preserve the best balance of species. The autumn flush can then be systematically rationed with the minimum of wastage by trampling and fouling.

One sees in this pasture the rationalising of feeding that has already been referred to. First of all, there is the safeguarding of quality, because high-producing stock, within the limits imposed by season, are always offered grass at the optimum stage of growth nutritionally. Secondly, there is a high proportion of surplus nutrients which are conserved, almost as a by-product of pasture control. Thirdly, there is an opportunity with these small independent grazing units of ringing the changes by management, top-dressing, and the use of special-purpose seed mixtures, if these are considered important, to give a high measure of flexibility.

Essentially this was the basis of the system of intensive paddock grazing that the late Andre Voisin demonstrated in Normandy some years ago and which now has many advocates in Britain. An important feature of the system is that it allows preferential treatment of stock that require the best available grazing. In its earliest form in New Zealand, the milking herd took the cream off the pasture, and dry stock following behind grazed the residue. Later a scheme was developed where the calves were grazed ahead of their mothers to give them an advantage of approximately 50 kg at the yearling stage over calves which were reared on the traditional system of a calf paddock which denied them the opportunity for reasonable development. This is a point to which we will return later.

THE RUAKURA EXPERIMENT

The Ruakura experiment on controlled versus uncontrolled grazing, already referred to, is one of the most thought-provoking studies in pasture management that has been attempted. Originally it was designed largely as a study of the influence of plane of nutrition on dairy cows maintained entirely on pasture. The pasturage was divided uniformly into equal areas to provide two farms. One farm system was based on controlled rotational grazing with subdivision, the conservation of surpluses, and the saving of autumn feed for late-winter grazing of newly-calved cows. At the outset of the experiment, it represented what most people considered to be a climax in grassland dairy farming.

Its partner farm had the same rate of stocking, the same sort of stock, and the same husbandry, except that there were only two fields, a night and a day enclosure with a portion of the latter cut off in the spring to make hay, which was the only form of supplementary winter feeding. This represented a slap-happy system of dairying, insofar as pasture management was concerned, but it is important to remember that all other aspects of management were good.

Average production after the first ten years of the trial was only 13 per cent higher on the controlled system than that for the uncontrolled system. It is not surprising that the result made those concerned wonder about the economics of a system based on close subdivision and intensive grazing. Detailed examination of the results and the conditions of the trial, however, reveal several important features which do not weaken, but rather strengthen, the case for controlled grazing, especially under British conditions.

The first point is that, though in good grass years there was very little difference between the systems, because there was no real stress on the cows, in bad grass seasons, with a delayed spring and summer drought, the difference widened to 25 per cent. A good grass year in New Zealand means good grazing for virtually ten months of the year and very little nutritional stress on stock even under intensive grazing conditions. A bad grass year is something much more akin to the conditions we usually have to put up with, especially in regard to length of winter.

IMPORTANCE OF STOCKING INTENSITY

Controlled grazing has a valuable insurance function in difficult years, because it is a method of preventing wide fluctuations in annual income. More than this, it gives

PLATE 7a

Rationing early spring growth of RvP Italian ryegrass using electric fencing.

PLATE 7b

High-density stocking of ewes and lambs on clean grazing.

Farmers' Guardian

PLATE 8

Good permanent pasture has many virtues in grass finishing.

confidence in building up the stocking rate on a farm. If one is coming out of the average winter with substantial reserves of hay and silage, the fear of over-stocking disappears.

This leads to the second feature of the trial. Both farms carried the same number of cows and followers at the rate of one cow-equivalent per 0·4 hectare. Though this was high, even on the existing New Zealand standards, on the controlled system it was still within the range where production did not suffer because of over-stocking. The point of this remark will be understood when it is stated that subsequent adjustments to the experiment, involving increases in stocking rates (but the elimination of followers), resulted in a reduction in yield per hectare on the uncontrolled farm, because the fall in yield per cow was not compenstated by the extra stock which were carried. This did not happen on the controlled farm, for, despite a small fall in production per cow, production per hectare rose to the remarkable figure of 12,716 litres of Jersey milk.

Another feature which helped to account for the smallness of the difference between the systems in the first ten years of the trial was that the cows on the controlled system were approximately 50 kg heavier than those on the uncontrolled. This extra weight used food that would otherwise have gone into milk, and it raised the maintenance requirements of the controlled herd. Here we see not only the importance of small animals under grazing conditions, but also evidence of the operation of diminishing returns in the feeding of dairy stock. As the plane of nutrition is raised, the proportion of nutrients that goes into milk tends to fall because more goes on the cow's back. Although these cows look well, and produce well, the extra production is not as great as it would be if there was a straight-line relationship between food input and milk output.

There is evidence from at least five other major New Zealand experiments that a high rate of stocking is more important than a high yield per cow in determining high production per hectare and this is borne out by the results of farm surveys. This does not imply that yield per cow is unimportant, nor that there are real dangers of over-stocking. Every effort must be made to improve cow yields by breeding and selection, disease control, and good husbandry, while nutritional stresses on the herd at critical times, such as immediately prior to calving and during peak lactation, must be minimised.

This brings us to what might be called the psychological effects of increasing stocking rate. Once a farmer is committed to a heavier stocking rate, he will make every effort he can to prevent waste and to increase pasture production by the several methods at his disposal so that his stock do not suffer.

The importance of high stocking rates is just as great in Britain as it is in New Zealand, and information is accumulating to support this view, not only in dairying but also in sheep production. It is a reasonable goal on a British dairy farm, with land of reasonable quality, to aim at a cow equivalent to 0·5 hectare of grassland with concentrates, either purchased or home-grown, being fed at a rate of not more than 1·5 tonnes per animal, unless the herd and its management are of exceptional quality. A corresponding standard in lowland fat lamb production is a stocking intensity of 15 ewes to a hectare of grassland devoted to the ewe flock, and effective lambing rate of not less than 1·65 lambs for every ewe put to the ram, and a concentrate use, including that fed to lambs, of 55 kg per ewe.

The fact that relatively few grassland dairy farmers in Britain achieve this sort of standard is attributable partly to poor pasture management, but also to the arbitrary ceiling that is put on farm carrying capacity by the accommodation available in buildings. If a 40 hectare grass farm has standings for thirty cows, and yards and boxes for a similar number of young stock, then there will be approximately a hectare to the cow-equivalent, and the tempo of grassland farming will be geared to this ratio.

One of the great advantages of the loose-housing system of

cow-keeping is the flexibility it gives to increase cow numbers, because one is not tied to a number corresponding to the availability of standings.

CASE FOR CONTROLLED STOCKING

It is stressed, however, that if one attempts a high rate of stocking in Britain with only a modest use of concentrates, then it is absolutely essential to have controlled grazing – either by permanent subdivision, which is appropriate on the all-grass farm, or by the use of electric fencing on the larger fields that are characteristic of alternate husbandry.

In this connection it may be said quite categorically that fold grazing, using the electric fence, especially if the precaution is not taken to back-fence, does not give any appreciable advantage over intensive rotational grazing, using paddocks.

The early experiments contrasting fold grazing with rotational grazing in this country indicated a 20–30 per cent production advantage in favour of the former system, but this difference was entirely accounted for by the increased stocking rates which were adopted for fold grazing. New Zealand experiments of a similar type took the precaution of equalising stocking rates, and there were no appreciable differences in milk yield per hectare. It is important to remember that the comparison was made with *intensive* rotational grazing and not *extensive* rotational grazing, where the herd is in the one field for a number of days. Compared with the latter situation, fold grazing is likely to be a much better proposition because of a reduction in waste by fouling and consequently a fuller utilisation of available herbage.

However, it serves little purpose to debate the merits of the two systems, which will in any case vary according to the circumstances of the farm. The all-important consideration is that there is a control of grazing to create a situation where a farmer can see weeks ahead in his grazing programme and be able to plan so that there is a sequence of quality grass always available for his herd. At the same time, he must be in a position to isolate surplus grass from his stock and conserve it so that winter carrying capacity is no longer a bottleneck limiting summer stocking to the point that there is serious under-utilisation.

TWO-SWARD SYSTEM OF MANAGEMENT

This system has acquired a lot of prominence on dairy farms over recent years, largely because of its advocacy by those who are interested in promoting nitrogen sales. Basically it represents an attempt to use one closely subdivided part of the farm for grazing and a second part for conservation, usually in the form of two or more silage cuts, with growth during the remainder of the season being grazed, generally by followers. It is by no means a new concept. Somerville when he laid down the Palace Lees manuring trial at Cockle Park in 1896 was doing no more than attempting to find the best method of increasing yields from fields that were used for hay year after year.

The perpetual hay-field fell into disrepute for a very good reason because repeated depletion of plant nutrients, without an adequate return of fertility, resulted in miserable crops that contained more herbs and weed grasses than species that are generally recognised as being useful. Now the wheel has taken a full turn, as it so often does in agriculture, and we are back to a two-sward system in a different guise. Fortunately it includes recommendations for adequate fertilising of pastures and this is important on those fields where there is an incomplete return of animal excrements.

The proponents of the two-sward system extol its simplicity. The grazing area is divided into 20–30 enclosures, the number varying according to taste and convictions as to how quickly the cows should return to the paddocks. Usually the herd occupies a paddock for a day and a night, and any grazing that is left behind is regarded as something for the next time until mid-season when there is generally a need to do some topping. Usually it is recommended that nitrogen is applied after each complete grazing so that there will be a good growth for the next visit by the herd and this largely accounts for the support the system gets from those in the nitrogen business.

The pro-arguments include the fact that there is no need to shift an electric fold fence either once or twice daily, and it is also claimed that there is less need for a dairyman to exercise his judgment as to how much or how little he will allow his herd every time he shifts this fence. It is also argued that there is a well-defined conservation area so that the whole utilisation programme, both grazing and conservation, can be planned at the beginning of the season.

There may be much to be said for the system for the not-so-good grassland farmer who still has a lot to learn about how he handles his pastures and his herd. It may appeal to the good farmer, who through pressure of other business, has to delegate responsibility of day-to-day management to someone else in whom he has not complete confidence, but it cannot be regarded as a top level approach to grassland dairy farming.

For our part we would be less critical about this system if there was much less variability in pasture, both quantitatively and qualitatively, over the season. Highly rigid systems of utilisation are not compatible with the dynamics of pasture growth and we prefer a more flexible approach where paddocks are sufficiently large that it is practicable to take conservation equipment into them when this is necessary. Such a size will necessitate the use of the fold fence at the height of the growing season in order to avoid waste of nutrients and also to give more scope for taking paddocks out of the grazing rotation for conservation purposes.

Nor do we favour the 'cookery book' concept of a defined conservation area. Apart from the fact that cutting, especially for silage, is a means of preserving a sequence of clean aftermaths over the summer, a point that has previously been stressed, there is the need to make decisions that match the vagaries of climate. A late spring will often necessitate a raid on an area that may have been earmarked for conservation or, conversely, a favourable spring may give an opportunity for building up fodder reserves.

The higher the stocking intensity, the more important it is to come out of the winter of an average year with reserves of fodder, so that there is something in hand for the occasional year when Nature is being difficult. In other words, one has to use one's head in top level grassland farming for there is no one recipe that fits the variety of circumstances that are encountered, especially when there are very high stocking intensities. There is really no satisfactory substitute for brains and a preparedness to use them to best advantage.

It is interesting to note that of the 34 high performance herds that figured in the Rex Paterson Memorial Study, entitled the *Contribution of Grass to Profitable Milk Production*, there were 21 that followed a two-sward system as opposed to 13 that favoured the alternative of cutting and grazing. The two-sward practitioners were mainly on large farms and some had a considerable element of cash crop production. Under such circumstances there will generally be a proportion of the grassland area which is too remote from the parlour for convenient use by the milking herd. Here the two-sward system can be a sensible arrangement but our preference is for the greater flexibility of combining mowing and grazing when this is a feasible proposition.

In the early seventies there was a limited advocacy of set stocking, where there is no attempt during the height of the growing season to restrict the grazing area of a dairy herd beyond the possible provision of night and day fields. Invariably this approach is based on a separate conservation area. Proponents argue that cows are more contented because there is less disturbance and there was no loss of production when the change was made from controlled grazing to set stocking. Why, it is argued, saddle yourself with the cost of subdivision and the management problems of controlled grazing when there is apparently very little to be gained from the latter system?

In effect the argument is a repeat of the controversy that followed the publication of results from the first ten years of the controlled versus uncontrolled grazing trial at Ruakura. The answer came for many in the severe summer drought that was experienced in 1976. Many practitioners of set stocking found the grazing pressures were such that they could only keep going by an expensive increase in concentrate feeding and by inroads into the silage and hay reserves for the following winter. However, in the Paterson study, 9 of the 34 herds adopted set stocking as opposed to 18 with some form of strip grazing and 5 who followed a conventional system of one-day paddocks.

GRAZING STORE CATTLE

The evidence on the different systems of stocking with store cattle, which are either to be reared as dairy replacements or are being fattened, is much more meagre than it is for milking cows or fat lambs.

Reference has already been made to the New Zealand system of rotating young calves on pastures ahead of the dairy herd. In the Ruakura trials Jersey calves reared in this way were nearly 50 kg heavier at nine months than their mates reared on the old method of set stocking in a calf field, where there was a deterioration of feed supplies because of highly selective grazing and a build-up of disease. The advantage was not purely one of weight, for the survival rate of rotationally-grazed calves was also much higher.

The early rearing stage in any class of stock is always important, and youngsters, whether they be lambs or calves, should never be used as tools of pasture management. It is a different matter with an in-calf heifer which is well grown. We do not want her to be too fat, and she can be made to work for her living without detriment to her subsequent performance, provided she is steamed up over the last six weeks of pregnancy.

The traditional feeder of beef cattle prefers a system of set stocking to all others, and attempts to equate grass growth and stock appetite by drafting in additional beasts until growth reaches a peak. Then he commences to lighten the load by drafting off beasts in the summer as they become prime. Occasionally a set number of cattle are put into a field in the spring and the adjustment is made by adding ewes and lambs in limited numbers so that the suitability of the pasture for cattle is not impaired.

There have been various attempts to strip-graze fattening cattle, but these have not been very successful. Whether this has been the fault of the system, or the fault of the people operating it, is not clear. The most general criticism, and it seems to be a valid one, is that feeding cattle are restless behind an electric fence, and restlessness is not compatible with a good liveweight gain.

Strip grazing is of value in a beef unit when handling foggage in the early winter for single-suckling cows. Here the aim is to maintain rather than fatten, and strip grazing will not only avoid waste from trampling, but will ensure a more even plane of nutrition during the period of utilisation. Rather than give a fresh break every day as in dairying, larger blocks are given, with the fence being moved every 4–5 days.

FAT LAMB PRODUCTION

Again, in fat lamb production the traditional method is non-rotational grazing at low rates of stocking, using cattle to control pasture, and it undoubtedly gives the best lambs. This was the finding in another comprehensive trial at Ruakura

which compared non-rotational grazing with rotational grazing at medium and heavy rates of stocking. The best lambs
were drafted off the set-stocked system at the lower rate of
stocking, but the greatest liveweight gains per hectare were
produced by the rotational high-rate treatment. Rotational
grazing at the lower rate give disappointing lambs, partly
because the pastures were not controlled in such a way as to
give the dense leafy pasture which is the best sort of food for
ewes and lambs. The general conclusion at the end of the trial
was that a system of set stocking was preferable where there
was a relatively low stock density, but it was advisable for the
farmer who was aiming to intensify fat lamb production to
adopt rotational grazing.

Since 1980, with changes in grading standards of slaughter
lambs which now penalise heavy overfat carcasses, there is
greater scope for increasing stocking intensities of ewes and
their lambs provided steps are taken to minimise the impact of
internal parasites. The view that low-intensity set stocking
produces the best lambs is no longer valid in a financial climate
that requires the highest possible gross margin per hectare as
opposed to gross margin per ewe. On the face of things, it might
appear that there are now economic grounds for a revival of
creep grazing but this is unlikely because the effort required
will not, in the estimate of most sheep farmers, generate a
commensurate addition to income. A system involving some
rotation of grazing on clean pasture, provided the flock is not
subjected to a markedly saw-tooth fluctuation in its plane of
nutrition, seems to be a more likely development in the
intensification of fat lamb production.

One period of the year when rotational grazing of ewes is
unquestionably advantageous is during the late autumn and
winter, after mating has been completed. Usually at this period
there are stubbles which can be eaten out in succession before
they are ploughed, and then there are the fogs which remain
from cattle grazing. If the ewe flock is concentrated on each
pasture in turn, the cream of the grazing can be taken; anything

that has been fouled can be left a few weeks to freshen and provide another useful bite for the flock.

An additional advantage of such a system is that it gives a basis for planning a grazing programme, which is not possible where the ewes are spread thinly over all the grassland. Above all, it gives the opportunity of saving some reasonably good grazing, preferably on an old pasture, for the ewes as they come up to lambing. One can work ewes hard during the first two-thirds of pregnancy, but not over the last third, when foetal growth is at a maximum.

This is a typical example of the art of good stock husbandry, stressed at the beginning of this chapter as being essential if we are to make the best possible use of grass. It also exemplifies the way that stock can be used as tools in pasture improvement and nowhere is this better illustrated than by the system known as 'mob stocking', which is widely adopted on hill sheep farms in New Zealand. The combination of aerial top dressing, closer subdivision of the farm and the concentration of ewes on a succession of paddocks over the period following mating until just before lambing, has transformed huge areas of hill grazing to the point where the quality of pastures is comparable with those found on lowland farms.

Chapter 8

FOOD SUPPLIES AND STOCK APPETITE

In Britain the characteristic pattern of pasture growth, after a long period of winter dormancy, is a rapid increase in spring as soil temperatures move appreciably above 5 degrees C, which is the point at which plants start to grow. The spring flush is generally followed by a summer slump, which is partly attributable to the maturity of plants and, in most seasons, to a shortage of moisture. Favourable conditions in the autumn generally result in a second, but smaller, flush which tails away as cooler temperatures exert their effects. Except in the most favourable localities, there will be no appreciable growth from November until well into March.

The cyclical nature of pasture growth creates many problems for the grassland farmer. But it can be said as a general principle that his aim should be to try and obtain the maximum degree of utilisation as grazing. Any form of conservation has at least two costs. The first is that for labour and machinery, and the second derives from the considerable loss of nutrients involved in both haymaking and ensilage, even when the operations are undertaken efficiently. The average loss of nutrients in silage-making is certainly not less than 25 per cent, and it can be even higher in haymaking by the time the product is fed to stock.

EXTENSION OF GRAZING

It is important to remember that endeavours to extend the grazing season must be kept in an economic perspective. It is not impossible to grow pineapples on Snowdon, but it is not very sensible to do so, and certainly we do not want out-of-season grass to come into this category of effort. Neither do we want to punish pastures during very wet weather and impair their subsequent productivity in rash attempts to extend the grazing season. There is an old saying in the Midlands, that a bullock out on pasture during the winter months has five mouths.

The fat lamb producer obtains the best synchronisation of grass growth and stock appetite – if we except those fortunate people who can afford to purchase store cattle in the spring and sell them fat as feed fails. The ordinary run of farmers, and especially dairy farmers, are not in this position, and it is necessary that they arrive at the cheapest possible feeding programme consistent with good yields. With present price relationships, this boils down to ensuring that grass in its several forms makes the major contribution to feeding over twelve months of the year.

The principal methods of achieving this end are as follows:
(a) Selective top-dressing
(b) Use of special-purpose pastures
(c) Management
(d) Conservation of surplus grass
(e) Timing of lambing and calving

USE OF NITROGEN

Selective top dressing implies the application of nitrogenous fertilisers but, it is reiterated, these should be used only when other deficiencies have been made good. The application of nitrogen provides one of the most effective ways of extending the grazing season. The late-winter dressing, applied towards the end of February, in the south, and about a month later in the north, will give effective grazing 2–3 weeks earlier than normal. This comes about because available nitrogen is generally very low at the end of the winter, partly as a result of leaching of this nutrient, and partly because of the cessation of activity by soil micro-organisms concerned in the nitrogen cycle during the period of very low temperatures. Usually it is lack of nitrogen rather than temperature or moisture which limits growth in the earlier part of the spring.

Nitrogen treatments can be used throughout the growing season to keep up the continuity of grazing should this be necessary. Here one comes up against the conflict between bag nitrogen and clover nitrogen, and so it is essential to exercise a considerable amount of judgment. If clover is making a vigorous contribution, and there is ample grazing for foreseeable needs, there is no point in using bag nitrogen to stimulate growth.

Except for the growing body of dairy farmers who are practically ignoring the clover contribution and using very large quantities of nitrogen, it is best to adopt an opportunist attitude to this fertiliser during the main part of the growing season. In other words, to use it if it appears that the crop needs stimulation for either grazing or conservation.

Nitrogen has a much more definite function during late summer, because it provides a very effective means of stimulating the autumn flush to provide a bulk of feed which can be rationed well into the winter. Clean autumn grass in quantity will provide sufficient nutrients for the stale cow that has been in milk since the spring, but one can over-estimate its value for the freshly-calved cow, which should receive at least 1 kg of concentrates for every 5 litres of milk it is producing. This need not be a balanced dairy ration, because autumn grass of good quality is high in protein and so the nutritive ratio of the concentrate mixture can be a fairly wide one.

ROLE OF ITALIAN RYEGRASS

The use of nitrogen for stimulation of out-of-season growth is most effective when it is used in conjunction with Italian ryegrass, which has such a good growth performance both early and late in the year, as well as a capacity to remain green

fairly well into the winter. One of the most striking developments in pasture farming since the early fifties is the role of
Italian ryegrass. Its traditional use has been as a companion
for red clover in a one-year seeds mixture intended for hay
production, but now it is very widely used for grazing and
usually without the addition of clover.

There is nothing to match it for earliness and its capacity to
respond to nitrogen, while it is undoubtedly one of the best
grasses we have for stimulating milk yield. One of its virtues is
its palatability and on many occasions we have moved dairy
cows in late May from stemmy Italian ryegrass, which we
considered would be better conserved rather than grazed, to a
leafy general-purpose mixture and have then experienced a
drop in production. It is indeed a grass with many virtues – the
pity is that it is not a perennial.

The usefulness of Italian for early bite varies, to some
extent, according to its age and time of sowing. Undoubtedly
the earliest and best grazing in the spring comes from a stand
that has been established towards the end of the previous
summer which has been properly established before the end of
the growing season. Usually such a stand is full of vigour in the
following spring, but it suffers from the disability that it will
easily poach if the land is heavy and the spring is a wet one.

For this reason, it is wise to have a second stand of Italian
in its second year on consolidated land, which can provide
alternative early bite should the season be difficult. If one
sows one of the Italian ryegrass varieties recommended by the
National Institute of Agricultural Botany or the Scottish
Colleges of Agriculture in preference to one of the cheaper
strains, and manages the sward properly, it will thoroughly
justify its being kept into a second year in this manner. Usually,
after the spring grazing, it will respond to another nitrogen
dressing and give a useful cut of silage. It can then be broken
for kale or rape or, alternatively, if one prefers to do without
these crops, for another reseed of Italian, or possibly a long-
term ley.

An alternative sowing time for Italian is in the early spring, either as a direct reseed or in a cereal crop. We adopted this latter method in the cold north-east of England because we found it gave a great deal more elbow-room in planning grazing over the winter–early spring period. The direct reseed in the spring, whether it be Italian or a longer ley, gives a very valuable contribution in the summer, when production is tending to slump, but it gives nothing in April, which is usually a critical month for grass.

On a tillage farm, apart from its more conventional use, Italian ryegrass can be used as a catchcrop, undersown in a strong-strawed spring barley at a rate of about 25 kg of seed per hectare. If it is top-dressed with a 50–60 kg N per hectare immediately after the straw is removed it will give useful stubble feed to take the burden off the longer leys going into the winter. Again, with a similar nitrogen application in late February–early March, it will provide useful early grazing at a time when longer leys will benefit through being free of stock. As it has been cheaply established, which will usually be the case if a commercial Italian has been used, it can be given harsher treatment than would be appropriate for a direct seeding using an expensive strain of Italian. After its spring contribution it can be ploughed out so that the land can be given a part fallow before being sown to a forage crop such as rape, kale or turnips, or even to a long ley. This last option is particularly useful in late districts, such as in north-east England, where the harvest of spring-sown cereals is usually so protracted that it is seldom practicable to direct reseed a pasture in the autumn, except after a crop of early harvested spring barley.

RATES OF NITROGEN APPLICATION

There is no great conformity in the rates of nitrogen dressing used for early grazing. Generally they are in the range of 80–100 kg N per hectare though occasionally one finds farmers using dressings as high as 140 kg N. We suggest that it is wiser to split such massive dressings, for instance 80 kg N followed by 60 kg N after the first grazing, as cold wet conditions soon after the initial application could lead to heavy leaching of the soluble nitrogen and much of its value could be lost.

This raises the question of how early one can safely apply this first dressing. Except under the most favourable conditions, there appears to be no point in top dressing before the end of the second week in February in the south, and 2–4 weeks later in the north. Because we have such variations in the onset of favourable growth conditions from year to year, considerable judgement has to be exercised. Nor is there any point in top dressing all pastures intended for early bite at the one time. Not only can risks be spread by making a succession of dressings, but it is possible in this way to provide for a succession of grazing.

Usually the nearer we come to the point of ideal conditions for growth, the greater will be the growth response per unit of applied nitrogen. At the same time it is often a worthwhile risk to chance one's arm, so to speak, by top dressing a small area, perhaps enough for 15 days' grazing, the same number of days before one normally considers it prudent to make the main early-bite dressing.

EARLY GRAZING FROM LONG LEYS

Though Italian ryegrass gives the earliest grazing, this does not mean that it is impracticable to go for early bite from longer leys, especially those based on perennial ryegrass or timothy and meadow fescue. They are particularly responsive if they have been fairly recently established. Almost any seed mixture which has been established in the previous August will give excellent early bite in the following spring if it has received the appropriate nitrogen dressings. The main drawback against using such leys for early grazing is the risk of excessive poaching.

The growth performance of any pasture in the early spring is very much influenced by the treatment it receives in the previous autumn and winter. Hard continuous grazing at that time, especially if there is mild weather which keeps growth going, will impair spring production.

This brings us back to the point that, so far as the plant is concerned, the function of leaf is not to feed stock but to build up root reserves. A systematic closing up of the pastures in the autumn to produce a lot of leaf will serve two purposes. First, it will give a succession of grazing going into the winter, and secondly, it will build up root reserves to promote early spring growth.

This latter objective will not be secured, however, if back-end grazing is continuous. The aim should be to effect quick utilisation followed by rest, so as to avoid grazing the regrowth thrown up immediately after grazing. Such regrowth, how-ever, can be safely grazed once hard weather sets in and the pasture becomes dormant. In fact, a hard grazing at this time with sheep may be the right treatment for the ley that carries a fair amount of roughness in order to give a clean fresh start in the spring.

Spring growth can not only be impaired by continuous grazing in the previous autumn, but it can also suffer if the pasture goes into the winter in too proud a condition. This is especially true of Italian ryegrass, which can go to mush if it is too soft and leafy when the hard frosts commence. This effect is quite commonly seen in the spring in Italian ryegrass which has been fairly laxly grazed in the previous autumn. Usually the urine patches which have gone into the winter in a very proud condition will be bare of grass which has rotted away. One can see in this danger the importance of adopting a happy medium, by always grazing a pasture in the autumn before it gets dangerously proud, but at the same time avoiding the risk of over-grazing.

The building of the root reserves can be critical at other times of the year, and especially before the onset of the summer drought. Hard grazing impairs rooting systems, so it is wise to top-dress at least one field which has been cut for early silage as a reserve in case there is a June–July drought. If the drought does not materialise it can go for hay or a later cut of silage. However, if drought conditions ensue not only does it provide a useful bulk of grazing but, because it has been allowed to build up leaf, it will show a good recovery after this grazing.

Leys based on cocksfoot and Montgomery clover are especially valuable for this purpose on land that tends to dry out in the summer, and the same function can be served by a timothy/meadow fescue ley without cocksfoot on soils with better moisture-retention qualities. Perennial ryegrass is not very useful for this purpose because of its tendency to throw up a second crop of heads.

SPECIAL-PURPOSE LEYS

A few years ago it was fashionable to advocate the use of a wide variety of special-purpose pastures as part of the programme for providing leafy grazing over the season. The wisdom of this is in doubt, because it tends to make management too complicated, and it has the further disadvantage of giving too much in the way of bits and pieces when it comes to conservation, especially on the small farm. A silage clamp can easily become an American sandwich of different sorts of pasture, and this has many drawbacks, especially if self-feeding is adopted.

As a general policy, it is better to rely mainly on one sort of pasture, which can be based on any mixture considered to be suitable for the farm. It can be a timothy/meadow fescue mixture, a Cockle Park mixture, or even permanent grass, according to circumstances or preference. In most cases where conditions normally favour growth, sufficient flexibility can be secured by the management imposed on this main pasture type, and the inclusion of a limited area of Italian ryegrass in the grassland programme. In drier parts it is probably wise to include one special-purpose ley, for instance one based on lucerne with a suitable companion grass. It is the best insurance there is against drought, where irrigation is not feasible.

PLANNING PASTURE USE

Already a considerable amount has been written about the various management processes, apart from top dressing, which can be employed to arrange a sequence of good grazing – for example, the timing of cutting or grazing, the duration of resting, the planning of pasture estabishment, and so on. The important issue is to plan ahead with a real purpose. Herein lies the importance of some subdivision of pasture land, whether it be with temporary or permanent fencing. Only in this way can the potential of grassland be realised.

It has been stressed in the last chapter that a high rate of stocking is a key to a high level of production. But a high rate of stocking makes it doubly important to look ahead so that there will not be a scarcity at critical times. When growth starts to fail there must be reserves of feed ahead of stock – in the form of hay and silage, or grass which is saved *in situ*. If the needs cannot be met by grass in one of its forms, then one must turn to supplementary crops, but it is wise to keep these to the minimum because, in general, they are a relatively dear source of nutrients.

One final point in securing as close an approximation between the production of grass nutrients and the requirements of stock relates to timing of calving or lambing. Unless a farm is geared to enter the very limited market for early lamb, it is better to lamb down about a month before active pasture growth commences. The immediate needs of the ewes at lambing time will be met by pastures which have been rested from the end of the previous autumn, supplemented with roots, hay and concentrates. The aim is to have the flock coming to the point of maximum appetite at the time of maximum availability of grazing.

A similar situation holds with summer milk production from pasture, except that it is wise to arrange calving at least 6–8 weeks in advance of the availability of grazing. The cow calved in January–February, if she starts her lactation in good condition, can make good use of hay, silage and limited concentrates in the interim before grass is available. Provided a special effort is made to cater for the summer gap, production from grass will be sustained at a reasonably high level till the end of the autumn flush, when the cow will normally be dried off to be wintered mainly on hay and silage.

The April–May calver, on the other hand, may reach a higher peak in milk yield, but invariably her lactation will peter off at about the same time as the cow that has calved two months earlier. April to July are bad months for calving cows which are fed largely on pasture, because invariably they suffer from foreshortened lactations.

For the farmer who remains a winter-milk producer, especially in eastern districts, the best calving time seems to be the 6–8 weeks up to the middle of October, because this, among other things, will result in the cow being dry during the mid-summer period. The autumn flush of grass can also be fully exploited, and when the cows are stale at the end of the winter there is the stimulus of spring pasture to level out the lactation curve. Unquestionably, cows calving at this time in the drier counties of Britain have the best lactation performances, and it is from these areas, with their supplies of bedding straw and home-produced concentrates, that we should largely expect most supplies of winter milk.

There is much to recommend a fairly compact pattern of calving and this is particularly the case in dairying but it is also advantageous with a single-suckling herd. In the latter instance, apart from being able to adopt the same management pattern for the whole herd, which can be treated as one unit, there is the considerable benefit of having a reasonably uniform bunch of calves. A producer–retailer in dairying may be forced into a policy of both spring and autumn calving in order to maintain the necessary supplies for his retail business but a wholesale producer has no restrictions of this nature. If he adopts block calving either in the autumn or the late winter he and his dairy staff have one period of the year when the bulk of the herd is dry and there is some respite from the daily demands of milking. Not only is it possible to treat the milking herd as a unit in respect of such matters as the quality of offered grazing or levels of supplementary feeding but also there are uniform groups of replacement stock at the various stages of the rearing process.

Chapter 9

AUTUMN-SAVED PASTURE FOR WINTER GRAZING

Although it is well recognised that autumn pastures do not compare with spring and early summer growth in respect of feeding value or palatability, nevertheless it can be of considerable importance on stock farms, particularly on well-drained soils which will carry grazing stock well into the year's end without serious damage from poaching. Certainly under these circumstances, it is worthwhile for many farmers to make a determined effort to provide useful grazing as far into the winter as is practicable. Among other things, for instance, the protein of autumn grass is of greater value to a milking herd than that provided by a typical silage and so in this sense at least it is concentrate-sparing.

New Zealand farmers with their highly seasonal production systems have recognised the importance of what they term ASP or autumn-saved pasture. It is common practice on sheep farms rearing flock replacements to have a so-called hogget block, which will be grazed by cattle and then laid up in the early autumn to provide clean grazing for wintering ewe lambs that seldom receive any form of supplementary feeding. However, it is on dairy farms where autumn-saved pasture has its greatest importance, though fat lamb producers will often make some effort to save autumn-grown grass for ewes that are lambing in advance of pasture growth in the spring. Generally the management plan is one of withholding some of the autumn flush from dry sheep or from the spring-calving cows that are coming to the end of lactation so that it is available as stock come into full production at the end of the winter. The importance of the practice arises from the economic circumstances of New Zealand farming where prices are such that it does not normally pay to feed concentrates even to freshly-calved dairy cows, let alone to lambing ewes.

New Zealand farmers, especially those in the lowlands of the North Island, have the very considerable advantage of short winters and an absence of prolonged frosts characteristic of British winters. In consequence there is comparative freedom from winter-burn and the feeding value of the pasture is well sustained. We cannot follow New Zealand practice in full because of the length and severity of our winters. Nevertheless in more favoured districts climatically, such as south-west Britain and southern Ireland, we can go part of the way by making certain there is appreciable grazing available for cattle well into the autumn or extending effective grazing for sheep into the New Year. But this will necessitate a decision to husband grass in the late summer so that reserves are created for the back-end of the year.

The starting point in the process is a complete eating out of pastures in August and early September. Among other things this will result in a clean start so that only quality grazing is saved and also it creates the conditions which favour the dominance of desirable species such as perennial ryegrass rather than Yorkshire fog. A third benefit is that of turning rough feed into dung and urine to maintain the fertility cycle. Applied nitrogen will normally be necessary to ensure an adequate growth under British conditions where the contribution from white clover virtually disappears by the middle of September. Where one is dealing with a pasture with an appreciable clover content 75 kg N per hectare will usually be adequate but a grass-dominant pasture, for instance one based entirely on ryegrass, will justify a dressing of the order of 100 kg N. The response from applied nitrogen diminishes with the advance of autumn and applications after mid-September will only be justified in favourable situations with the persistence of reasonably warm conditions. In most districts of Britain one should aim to apply these autumn dressings of nitrogen by the first week of September in order to maximise response.

SPECIES FOR FOGGAGE

There is little doubt that when it comes to quality foggage Italian and hybrid ryegrasses are in a class by themselves, provided they are grazed before burning frosts set in for they are not frost-hardy, particularly when they are in a lush state. If a stand is getting proud early in October it may be advisable to take the top off it with the first frosts and then subject it to a more complete defoliation later in the autumn. In milder southern districts these ryegrasses should give good grazing well into December and still retain their propensity for stimulating the flow of milk. It is reiterated, however, that one does not want to be too greedy with stands of Italian or a hybrid like Sabel in the back-end by subjecting them to over-grazing, particularly with sheep, or excessive poaching, because this could impair their productivity in their more important subsequent role of providing quality grazing in the early spring.

Pastures based on timothy/meadow fescue mixtures are excellent for back-end grazing for they maintain palatability and are comparatively resistant to winter-burn. If such a mixture, which usually has an appreciable clover component, is closed by the end of August it will normally give a good grazing by the end of September. If it is closed again after this grazing there will usually be sufficient regrowth over the next six weeks to provide good grazing for a dairy or suckler herd by mid-November and this final grazing will be of benefit to the sward in that it will prevent any tendency to rankness and consequent openness in the pasture.

Though the improved varieties of perennial ryegrass that are now available exhibit good autumn growth, nevertheless if pastures based on them become very rank they are liable to go to mush with the first severe frosts. Generally if there is any hint of proudness in a ryegrass pasture it is advisable to graze it before the end of October. Any regrowth that is made seems to stand frosts much better than the earlier growth and it will normally provide useful grazing especially for sheep in December–January.

Cocksfoot gives more bulk than any other species, with the possible exceptions of Italian ryegrass and tall fescue, when it is laid up for foggage. It must, however, be top dressed and left ungrazed at least by the end of August if one is aiming for a reasonably full crop. Cocksfoot is prone to winter-burn but under conditions of high fertility there is usually a reasonable proportion of green material, though this is steadily reduced with the advance of winter. Cocksfoot foggage will have a feeding value in January approximating to that of average hay and as such will provide useful fodder for out-wintered store cattle but no more than this. Even if it is utilised well before the winter sets in cocksfoot foggage is not recommended for a milking herd.

When pastures containing cocksfoot, for instance one based on a Cockle Park mixture, is laid up for foggage year after year it will almost inevitably become cocksfoot dominant and there will be a loss of clover. If Yorkshire fog is a component of a sward it too will achieve dominance at the expense of more preferred species with repeated laying up for foggage. New Zealand experience suggests that it is advisable to ring the changes and not save autumn pasture year after year from the same field. Hard grazing into the winter, on the other hand, will restore the balance in favour of clover and the more prostrate grass species like ryegrass.

VALUE OF LUCERNE LEYS

In the late forties, when the Grassland Research Institute was still located on heavy clay land at Drayton in Warwickshire, workers there developed an interesting forage-foggage combination in the form of lucerne and cocksfoot in alternate drills about 300 mm apart. The intention was that it should provide two or three cuts for conservation, depending on local conditions, with the last being taken by mid-August. A dressing of 60–70 kg N/hectare was then applied to provide growth for grazing in mid-winter behind an electric fence, when the lucerne rows had died back. It was remarkable how cattle followed those lucerne rows when grazing, thus minimising damage to the cocksfoot drills. The dormant lucerne appeared to suffer few ill effects from poaching for there was strong growth in the following spring. With hard grazing of the cocksfoot in the winter a good balance of the two species was maintained for a number of years and this was a notable achievement on the heavy clay at Drayton.

Like several interesting techniques that were developed in the immediate post-war period the idea did not take on. The growing of lucerne is not favoured on heavy land farms with out-wintered suckler cows, which are the class of animal that would make best use of such foggage. Beef men relying to any degree on foggage for their cows or store cattle are more likely to employ general purpose pastures containing cocksfoot because of their greater flexibility. Indeed with greater mechanisation of grass conservation especially silage and the swing to in-wintering of horned stock, especially on heavy land, farmers generally are not now as concerned with cattle grazing in the dead months of the year as they were at the time of the Drayton trials.

Nevertheless on free draining land such as gravels, lucerne leys, especially those in combination with timothy and meadow fescue which are our preference as companion grasses, can not only be an excellent source of winter fodder and a reserve in the event of a summer drought but they can also make a useful contribution to early winter grazing. It is important in promoting the survival of a lucerne stand to build up root reserves from about the end of August until the cessation of growth which usually coincides with the onset of light frosts about the middle of October. At this point stock may as well have the remaining lucerne growth as the frosts. In the meantime there will be an appreciable growth in the companion timothy and meadow fescue which both retain greenness and a high measure of their nutritive value until well into the autumn.

PERMANENT PASTURE

Something must be said for the special place that old grassland, either a permanent pasture or a long ley, has in providing useful grazing during the winter months. It is especially valuable where there is a sheep flock lambing before there is much pasture growth. Too often the old grass on a farm is not allowed to make as full a contribution as it is capable of to winter keep, because it is less vulnerable than young grass to the ill effects of winter poaching and so has to carry an unduly heavy burden of winter stocking. When a farmer has switched to the in-wintering of his flock from the turn of the year until after lambing he is better able to appreciate the usefulness of well-managed old grass, especially in that interim between lambing and the onset of grass growth.

The autumn management of old grass that is required to make a significant contribution to grazing in the tail end of winter should be such as to avoid poaching or any opening up of the sward as the result of being excessively proud. It should go into the winter as a dense leafy sward that will not be liable to go yellow at its base. Many of the components of permanent pastures, for instance *Poa trivialis* and *Poa pratensis*, are winter-green species under conditions of high fertility and maintain their feeding value reasonably well despite low temperatures. It can be especially valuable for out-wintered ewes in that month just before lambing when appetite for bulky foods like hay or silage becomes jaded and there is danger of pregnancy toxaemia. It is so valuable that a farmer is justified in utilising such a grazing reserve by an on-and-off system where the flock has access to it for about two hours daily to extend its availability.

RELEVANCE OF OUT-OF-SEASON GRAZING

In 1960, when the first edition of this book was being prepared, the provision of back-end and winter grazing had a much greater justification in the planning of grassland production and utilisation than it has today. Factors contributing to this change in emphasis are first, the wider availability of labour-efficient in-wintering facilities for both beef and dairy cattle and, second, changes in fodder provision and conservation, in particular the greater emphasis on silage which is now a much more reliable feeding stuff than the unpredictable and sometimes very dubious product that passed for silage in the period immediately following the war.

Today there are many grassland farmers, especially in dairying, with convenient in-wintering facilities including self or easy feeding silage, who are much happier to divide their farming year into two distinct phases: one when conditions favour grass growth when the main reliance is on grazing and the other from the late autumn till the spring when the herds' bulk food requirements are principally met by high quality silage. Provided it is well organised and there are ample reserves of silage to last out to the spring it is a simple straightforward system that does not require special purpose pastures for early or late bite, while it is also virtually insulated from weather conditions in the worst months of the year when poaching can do irreparable harm to pastures.

One must agree with farmers, particularly those with autumn calving herds on strong land in the later grassland regions, that such a policy makes a lot of sense. However, there is another aspect of significance in the argument, namely that conserved grass, especially if it is of high quality, is comparatively expensive food because unlike grass as grazing it not only carries the cost of conservation but also the sometimes considerable toll of nutrient losses inherent in the operation. On top of this there is the cost involved not only in feeding silage and either disposing of slurry that cannot these days be flushed into a stream, or of additional straw where stock are bedded down in yards. Efforts to extend the grazing season have a considerable relevance in those areas of Britain which are favourable to late season grazing. They have greater justification too where the main effort is in summer milk production and in suckled-calf production. Though housing is becoming more common with the latter class of stock, especially if the herd is dominantly autumn-calving, most farmers not only prefer to calve down on pasture but also to keep cows and calves out of yards until such time as the risk of scouring is minimised, for this is a serious hazard with young calves in yards

There is no great point, however, in keeping cattle intended for winter fattening in yards out at pasture much later than the middle of October. They should come into their winter quarters before the stage is reached where pasture is doing little good for them and they are doing positive harm to pasture, which in a mixed stocking system is better utilised by sheep. When feeding cattle, particularly those of dairy origin, come to a stage where they are principally growing hide and hair, as can easily happen in the late autumn where apparent plenty in grazing is not necessarily synonymous with adequate nutrition, it takes a lot of subsequent feeding to bring back the bloom they have lost.

Chapter 10

HERBAGE PLANTS – SPECIES AND VARIETIES

Despite the infinite diversity in the composition of natural pastures relatively few species have a significant commercial value. Sown seed mixtures normally contain one or more of the following: perennial ryegrass, Italian ryegrass, timothy, cocksfoot, meadow fescue and white or red clover.

Most programmes of grassland intensification are however based on perennial ryegrass, and it is this species which currently accounts for about 80 per cent of grass seed sales. At present it is difficult to foresee a role for the other sown species – cocksfoot, timothy and meadow fescue – although they may be valuable for some special uses, for example cocksfoot's ability to withstand dry conditions. Even some of these special requirements could eventually be fulfilled by ryegrass varieties bred specifically for that purpose.

SPECIES ATTRIBUTES

The farmer's ideal grass species would combine a number of features, each developed to a high degree. The most important of these are:

(a) Yield
The total annual production and its seasonal distribution will directly influence the stock-carrying capacity of the pasture, however, species differences represent only a minor part of yield variation. The effects of environment and management account for over 90 per cent of the total yield differences in grass production. In terms of seasonality of production the herbage

species differ quite markedly, the ryegrasses showing clear advantages in both spring and autumn production. All grass species grow relatively well in late spring and early summer.

(b) Persistence

Persistence is a most important aspect when the cost of sward renewal is taken into account. Once the sward is established its longevity will depend on the standard of management imposed and on the inherent persistence of the constituent varieties. Late heading varieties with a high tillering capacity, producing a dense sward, are the most persistent types. Providing that the basic requirements of drainage, adequate lime and fertiliser use and suitable grazing management are met then these varieties of perennial ryegrasses should last indefinitely.

(c) Palatability

Grazing animals, especially sheep, can be highly selective in their choice of herbage. Timothy and meadow fescue, traditionally regarded as very palatable species, are losing favour and are being replaced gradually by tetraploid ryegrasses. These also improve sward palatability but thrive under more intensive management regimes. The palatability of diploid ryegrasses is good for most of the year but certain varieties can become less acceptable to grazing stock, especially during the midsummer period.

(d) Reliability

With greater capital investment in livestock farming systems more demands are placed on grassland and consequently reliable production becomes imperative. This means that varieties have to be capable of establishing themselves rapidly, overcoming moisture stress and cold conditions and resisting pests, diseases and weed infestation. While no single species or variety is likely to be superior in all these aspects perennial ryegrass clearly demonstrates an all-round adaptability which accounts for its overwhelming popularity.

A GUIDE TO HERBAGE VARIETIES

This guide is based on the NIAB Leaflets of the *Recommended Grasses and Herbage Legumes.** It is by no means an exhaustive list but describes some of the popular varieties as well as some recently introduced.

Tetraploid varieties

The tetraploid Italian and perennial ryegrasses are distinguished by their broad, dark green leaves and their larger but fewer tillers. They have a higher water-soluble carbohydrate content than diploid varieties. A slightly lower dry matter content and thicker cell walls means that they need longer wilting for silage and hay crops.

Although they are generally less persistent than diploids they are very palatable and are well-suited for inclusion in seed mixtures for any intensive grass system.

Perennial ryegrass

The range of performance of perennial ryegrass varieties is wide especially in respect of heading date, persistence and winter hardiness.

Very early and early

Varieties in this category grow early in spring and are generally well-suited to conservation. However they tend to have poorer persistence than varieties with a later heading date.

The Dutch variety, Frances, introduced in 1977 combines early growth and high yields with a good level of persistence, while other relatively persistent early varieties are Monta and Barlano.

Intermediate

Talbot and Barlenna are well-established intermediate varieties.

* The Scottish Colleges of Agriculture have a similar list of varities which they recommend for their conditions.

Talbot is suitable for conservation since it maintains a high level of digestibility for several cuts, while Barlenna makes less spring growth but has a high degree of persistence and is a better grazing variety.

Fantoon is a tetraploid variety introduced in 1981 which combines high yield with resistance to the disease crown rust and also has a high water-soluble carbohydrate content. Its persistence is relatively good for its type.

Late and very late

The late heading varieties form the backbone of the long-term ley. They are generally leafy and persistent and have the ability to withstand the stresses imposed by intensive grassland systems.

Melle is still a difficult variety to better in this group, being very persistent and a particular favourite with the dairy farmer. Several other continental varieties have similar features to Melle, these include Compass, Wendy, Lamora, Perma and Preference.

The tetraploid variety Meltra which was bred from Melle, has given outstanding yields and is very persistent for a tetraploid. It has replaced timothy in many seed mixtures because of its good palatability and its ability to withstand intensive management.

Parcour, first listed in 1979, has excellent persistence and winter hardiness and has proved valuable as a constituent of upland swards.

Italian ryegrass

Italian ryegrass is notable for its early spring growth and its high yield potential but is unlikely to last for longer than 18–24 months. The species is particularly prone to several phyto-pathogens, especially leaf blotch, mildew and ryegrass mosaic virus. In areas where these diseases are troublesome the tetraploid varieties are likely to perform better than the diploid varieties.

Italian

RvP has proved itself the best yielding variety and also shows good persistence. However its palatability can be poor especially during the second half of the growing season. Optima and the high-yielding Whisper are the only other diploids whose persistence is comparable to RvP. Both these varieties are more winter hardy than RvP.

In general the tetraploid Italian ryegrasses suffer from poor persistence and most are suitable for one-year leys only. Of these the Danish variety Wilo has the best persistence and winter hardiness.

Hybrid ryegrass

Hybrid ryegrasses have been available for many years but these were the diploid forms whose impact did not compare with the tetraploid hybrids which were introduced in the early 1970s. For its work in breeding the new crosses the Welsh Plant Breeding Station was awarded the Queen's Award for Technological Achievement in 1976.

The hybrids combine some of the out-of-season growth of Italian ryegrass with some of the sward density and persistence of perennial ryegrass. The recommended hybrids are Augusta and Sabel, both varieties with good persistence and winter hardiness. Sabel is somewhat better suited to conservation than Augusta and has better all-round resistance to diseases.

Timothy

Timothy is especially suited to heavier soils and wetter areas of the country. Although its yield contributions are not high in comparison with ryegrass, it improves the acceptability of the sward to livestock and it is very winter hardy. It still has a role on the less intensive farm in higher rainfall areas but with increasing levels of applied nitrogen and higher stocking rates it is being replaced by the tetraploid ryegrasses.

Goliath is an early variety with very good persistence and high yields. Olympia and Aberystwyth S.48 are both persistent late heading varieties, the latter being especially useful as a constituent of seed mixtures for marginal and upland areas.

Cocksfoot

A species whose usefulness is limited to areas of severe moisture stress, cocksfoot now accounts for less than 5 per cent of seed sales. The newer varieties are more palatable than their predecessors but some tend to be less winter hardy. The recent introductions include Sparta, Cambria and Barata.

Other grasses

Meadow fescue and red fescue each have a minor role for special circumstances. Meadow fescue is most frequently sown with timothy and white clover, neither of these grasses being as aggressive as ryegrass, and allows good clover establishment. The red fescue variety Aberystwyth S59 has proved very successful on the exposed slopes of Welsh uplands, its winter hardiness and spring growth being outstanding under these harsh conditions.

New developments include the breeding of several varieties of brome grasses. These provide short duration crops which have very good out-of-season growth.

White clover

Varieties of white clover are classified according to leaf size; they range from the small-leaved varieties such as Aberystwyth S184 to the medium-large leaved Blanca and Sabeda. In many regions their performance is reduced by clover rot infections. This is a fungal disease which also affects red clover and virtually all clover varieties suffer reduced yield and persistence when grown in infected soils. Where the disease is known to be present then varieties with a good degree of resistance should be selected.

The small-leaved white clover varieties have a very prostrate, creeping growth habit and are the most persistent and hardy types. They thrive under intensive grazing and low

PLATE 10a

*A home-made heavy roller which will follow the
contours of the ground. This is extremely useful
for summer reseeds, as it shatters surface clods
and gives a really firm finish—a vital factor in
securing successful late-season establishment.*

PLATE 10b

*Cockle Park Jerseys grazing behind an electric
fence.*

nitrogen fertiliser use and are ideal for sheep pastures. Aberystwyth S184 has been extensively used on upland areas and is tolerant of these poorer conditions; however, both this variety and Kent Wild White are susceptible to clover rot. Pronitro, a slightly larger leaved variety, shows good clover rot resistance.

At the other end of the range, the medium-large leaved clovers are much taller growing plants with longer leaf stalks. Thus they are more effective in withstanding the effects of nitrogen than smaller leaved varieties. However, their persistence is not so good and they require more lenient grazing. In general these varieties may be used on grassland systems where up to about 250 kg/hectare of nitrogen are applied annually, although it should be remembered that their persistence is also influenced by moisture availability and by the grazing or cutting management imposed. Of the varieties in this group, Blanca yields well and also shows good resistance to clover rot. Olwen, Sabada and Kersey give particularly high yields except in the presence of clover rot.

The medium-small leaved clovers have features which are intermediate relative to those of the other two groups. The best known of these varieties are Aberystwyth S100 and the New Zealand bred Grasslands Huia.

The current choice of white clover varieties is influenced as much by their availability as by any agronomic superiority. Seed supplies of most British-bred varieties are very limited and of course expensive, while Huia for example is relatively plentiful and considerably cheaper. The pattern of usage of white clover varieties, which has remained steady in recent years, shows that Grasslands Huia accounts for almost two-thirds of seed sales, Danish varieties such as the medium-large leaved Milkanova represent about a quarter of the sales, leaving the British-bred varieties with about a sixth of the market. In the development of new white clover varieties, it is clear that seed yielding potential is an area which requires particular attention.

Red clover

Red clover varieties fall into two main groups, namely the early red clovers (previously known as broad red or double-cut red clovers) and the late red clovers (traditionally called late-flowering red clovers). The late red clovers have lost popularity in recent years, their main use being for medium-term leys for cutting. The early red clovers will generally last for two seasons, allowing up to four cuts per season. They have the advantage of being able to yield up to ten tonnes per hectare of dry matter at a low fertiliser cost. Some of the problems of ensiling the crop may be overcome by wilting and the use of suitable additives.

Red clover varieties may suffer from clover rot and also from stem eelworm and unfortunately none of the current varieties are resistant to both these problems. The introduction of tetraploid varieties has produced a significant improvement in yield performance and in clover rot resistance as compared with traditional diploid varieties. Tetraploids such as Redhead and Deben now set the standard for these particular qualities. On stem eelworm infested land the tetraploid Norseman or the diploids Sabtoron and Quin are the most suitable varieties.

Chapter 11

GRASS SEED MIXTURES

The opinions of grass farmers range widely as to the importance of choice of seed mixtures. Some maintain that the other management inputs for example nitrogen fertiliser, are the only criteria that are worthy of consideration. Other, possibly more discerning, practitioners place great emphasis on varietal differences which make each one suitable or unsuitable for their own requirements.

While it is true that many varieties are sufficiently versatile that they may be used in a wide range of circumstances, many special needs are clearly recognised. This allows specific recommendations to be drawn up for each type of grass and livestock enterprise.

In designing a herbage seed mixture there are four main factors to consider. The first is the intended duration of the ley. The basic choice is between a short-term ley of up to three years' duration and a long-term ley intended for at least six years. For the short-term ley the basic requirements are rapid establishment, a high yield potential and a long growing season. Italian and hybrid ryegrasses are ideally suited for this purpose, while inclusion of an early perennial ryegrass will help to extend the life of the pasture. These types of sward prove ideal for early grazing and for conservation.

The long-term ley demands that all the constituents have good persistence. Varieties which die out after two or three years will simply encourage sward deterioration through infestation of weeds. The basis of the long-term ley is therefore late-heading, high-tillering varieties, but it must be remembered that their longevity is very much influenced by the management they receive.

The second factor to consider in choosing a seed mixture is

the compatibility of the varieties. In general, mixtures should consist of grass and clover varieties which are compatible in growth pattern and growth habit. Whereas Italian ryegrass was normally included in many proprietary mixtures intended for long-term use, this practice has now declined. It is now recognised that the vigorous growth of the Italian species will suppress the more persistent varieties which are the most valuable in the long term.

The heading dates of the varieties in a mixture should be over a narrow range especially if the intention is to cut the sward for silage or hay. It is much easier to manage and to maintain swards where the heading date can be accurately predicted than swards in which the constituents head over a long period. In leys intended for grazing the range of heading dates should be no more than about fourteen days, while in leys primarily intended for cutting the range should be seven days or less.

Thirdly, consideration should be given to the use of the ley. While the intended purpose of some swards may be unclear it should be possible to predict whether a field will be mainly used for grazing or for cutting. Where grazing will be the main use, the best suited are the late and also the intermediate varieties, these produce swards which are leafy and densely tillering. Leys intended mainly for cutting may be based on early, intermediate or late varieties depending on the intended life of the sward; however, the more erect growth of early and some intermediate varieties will produce the better type of sward for cutting.

Finally the environmental conditions need to be considered. If varieties have reasonable resistance to disease and winter damage then there are few limitations to their distribution in the United Kingdom. The main restrictions are on exposed areas of high altitude or those suffering from regular moisture shortage. In the former case winter hardiness becomes a major requirement. On soils which suffer serious drought then herbage species such as cocksfoot or lucerne should be considered.

SEED MIXTURE RECOMMENDATIONS

The recommendations are given for typical livestock systems. The varieties used are to some extent interchangeable; for example a late heading perennial ryegrass may be replaced with another similar variety.

Hill land

These are swards which will be grazed, mainly by sheep and occasionally by cattle. The fertiliser input is likely to be under 100 kg of nitrogen/hectare/annum. The main requirements are persistence and winter hardiness. This mixture may thus be based on Parcour or Aberystwyth S23 perennial ryegrass and a small-leaved white clover such as Aberystwyth S184. The inclusion of Aberystwyth S59 red fescue depends on the harshness of the location. Aberystwyth S48 timothy is included for its hardiness and palatability.

Parcour perennial ryegrass	14 kg/hectare
Aberystwyth S48 timothy	4 ,,
Aberystwyth S59 red fescue	5 ,, (optional)
Aberystwyth S184 white clover	2 ,,

Marginal land

These are essentially livestock rearing areas. They are typically the high rainfall regions of the west and north, nevertheless their inherently thin brown earth soils will suffer some drought effects periodically. Long-duration leys are desirable under these conditions and the Cockle Park type ley is especially suitable. This is based on persistent varieties of perennial ryegrass, cocksfoot, timothy and white clover. The cocksfoot will demand careful grazing management to prevent it becoming too dominant.

Barlenna perennial ryegrass	8 kg/hectare
Preference perennial ryegrass	8 ,,

Barata cocksfoot	5 kg/hectare
Aberystwyth S48 timothy	3 ,,
Aberystwyth S100 white clover	1 ,,
Aberystwyth S184 white clover	1 ,,

Dairy systems

In general dairy farms are stocked more intensively and the demands made of pastures are more specific. It may be prudent to cultivate a range of pasture types from those based on early, to intermediate, to late heading varieties. This provides a sequence of grazing and cutting swards as the season progresses.

The early spring growth may be provided by leys based on short-term Italian and hybrid ryegrasses. On well-fertilised, good grass growing sites these may yield up to 17 tonnes of dry matter per hectare per annum if cut three or four times. Since they require reseeding at intervals of between one and three years they are best grown on land which is easily cultivated. Inclusion of early perennial ryegrass varieties, for example Barlano or Frances, will improve the duration of these swards.

Short-term ley for early bite and conservation:

RvP Italian ryegrass	10 kg/hectare
Augusta hybrid ryegrass	12 ,,
Barlano perennial ryegrass	6 ,,

For the intensive paddock or set-stocked grazing systems, where nitrogen levels of 350 kg/hectare or more are used annually, perennial ryegrasses with the highest level of persistence are required. A mixture based on diploid and tetraploid varieties such as in the example given below would be ideal. Clover is excluded as it is unlikely to survive under these conditions.

Lamora perennial ryegrass	7 kg/hectare
Melle perennial ryegrass	7 ,,
Meltra (tetraploid) perennial ryegrass	8 ,,

Intensive beef production systems

Swards which are suitable for fattening beef cattle on grass require a high degree of palatability and steady seasonal growth. These requirements may be met by a blend of intermediate and late-heading perennial ryegrasses plus timothy and white clover.

Barlenna perennial ryegrass	12 kg/hectare
Compass perennial ryegrass	8 ,,
Olympia timothy	3 ,,
Aberystwyth S100 white clover	2 ,,

Lowland sheep

With stocking rates of up to 15 ewes/hectare persistent varieties are essential. As with swards suited for beef cattle, ewes and lambs demand a high degree of palatability. The inclusion of timothy and the persistent small-leaved white clover meets this requirement. The intermediate variety Talbot in the selection given below increases the earliness of the sward.

Talbot perennial ryegrass	6 kg/hectare
Lamora perennial ryegrass	12 ,,
Aberystwyth S48 timothy	4 ,,
Kent wild white clover	2 ,,

PLATE 11a

*Close-up of the seed coulters and cutting discs
on the front-and-rear-sprung drag arms of the
Moore Uni-drill. The discs open up a slot for
the seed to fall into, which allows direct reseeding
without disturbing the rest of the pasture. Although
primarily a seed drill, the Uni-drill can also be
used to direct drill cereals and crops such as
stubble turnips and kale.*

PLATE 11b

With chemical ploughing, using one of the new materials to destroy grass, a reasonably clear surface can be prepared. Over-sowing with grass and clover seeds can then be carried out with a sod-seeding machine such as the Howard Rotaseeder, seen here.

PLATE 12

Clover is an essential element of pastures on marginal land.

Chapter 12

PASTURE ESTABLISHMENT

The two principal methods of establishing a pasture are (a) undersowing of a cereal crop intended for harvest, and (b) direct reseeding with or without a grazing nurse crop which may be a cereal or a cruciferous crop like rape. A third, less usual, method which is in the nature of a compromise between these two is the undersowing of an arable silage mixture.

Of these methods quite the most popular, and equally the most suspect, is the first – namely the undersowing of a cereal crop. It is popular because it is cheap, in that the major costs of cultivation are carried by the cereal crop, and there is also the feeling of having one's cake and eating it, in that pasture establishment is a by-product of cash cropping.

The latter part of this argument is not without flaws. In the first place, there must be some sort of compromise between the needs of the corn crop and the needs of the establishing pasture. Usually, one adopts a lower rate of seeding and fertilising for the cereal with the result that the crop is below the potential of the land.

This is an important consideration, because yield is lost at the profit end of the operation. However, this is usually a minor consideration as compared with a much more serious loss arising from poor establishment of pasture, either because of competition for moisture in a dry season, or because of lodging and mechanical and other damage which may occur in unfavourable harvesting conditions. This danger is not so acute if one is sowing a cheap seeds mixture which is intended to have a very short life, but it may have serious consequences for a long-duration ley based on expensive seeds. Here there is usually a temptation to persevere with a half-failure in the hope that it will fill up. Usually it will fill up, not with sown species, but with volunteers which will impair the subsequent productivity of the pasture.

ARGUMENTS FOR DIRECT RESEEDING

The strongest argument advanced by the protagonists of direct reseeding is that there is a much greater certainty of getting a full establishment of the sown species. Certainly this is true if the job is done properly by attending to essential points in pasture establishment. They answer the objection that there is a loss of the grain crop by pointing out that there is a counter credit of valuable grazing in the establishment year of a spring reseed.

Provided it is sown before mid-April, there will be fresh grazing during the summer-gap period from June to August, when older pastures are losing quality. It is well recognised that there is no better stimulus to milk yields at this time of the year than a spring-established pasture. By the end of September such a pasture can quite easily have produced 4,500 litres of milk to the hectare, a substantial credit to set against the loss of a grain crop.

This raises another consideration affecting pasture establishment policy, namely the type of farm in question. If the farm is large and the grass use is extensive rather than intensive, as it is under normal conditions of fat lamb and beef production, the case for direct reseeding is not as strong as it is in the small dairy holding, where every effort is being made to make the most of grass by heavy fertilising and intensive grazing methods.

Not only is a spring reseed more valuable to the dairy farmer than it is to a fattener, but there is the subsequent consideration that intensive methods of managing pasture are only fully justified if the pasture is a good one. In other words, the more efficient a farmer becomes in using his grass, the stronger becomes the case for establishment by direct reseeding.

LATE SUMMER RESEEDING

One very cogent argument against direct reseeding in the spring is that land may be out of production for such a long time. If the previous crop is a cereal, this period can extend from August through to May. Even if undersowing is some-what faulty, at least it will give some useful stubble feed in the autumn, especially if it receives help in the form of applied nitrogen. It will also give keep in April, which on most farms seems to be the hungriest month of the year.

This counter-argument only applies if one follows the practice of direct reseeding in the spring. There are, however, the strongest grounds for advocating direct reseeding in the late summer as an alternative to undersowing or spring seeding. In the southern part of Britain, except on farms which are late because of their elevation, there is usually ample time to follow an early-harvested cereal crop with a direct reseed and to get a first-class establishment before the onset of winter.

Such a policy of pasture establishment has a great deal in its favour. In the first place one can aim at a full cereal crop without any fears about prejudicing the undersown seeds. Secondly, because the soil is warm in August, the grass and clover seedlings develop very quickly – in most autumns there will be a really worthwhile flush of growth within a month of seeding, and there will be vigorous growth well into the back-end. Thirdly, these late summer established leys are especially vigorous in the following spring, and so make a full contribution at a time of normal food shortage. On all scores, except that one loses the summer milk stimulus of the spring-sown ley in its establishment year, the case for direct reseeding in the summer, especially with a ryegrass ley, is so strong that it is surprising that the practice is not more widespread.

Two main arguments are advanced against late summer seeding. The first is that it is another job to clash with harvest, but rarely do we have a harvest season that is not interrupted by broken weather which gives the opportunity for the necessary cultivation.

The second objection refers to the difficulty of getting a satisfactory take of clovers and this can be very real if precautions are not taken. It is essential to let light into the sward, both in the autumn and again in the following spring. This latter period is especially critical, and on no account should one take hay or early silage from the field, though a cut of late silage is permissible if it is in the interests of the farm.

In our experience late-summer reseeding has always been satisfactory when sowing has been completed by the end of August, but there is a real risk of partial failure and with it a necessity for spring patching with later September seeding, especially with heavy soils.

In Kent, the reseed usually followed winter barley or oats, which are harvested earlier than wheat. Occasionally it followed vining peas, which in many respects is an ideal preceding crop because the land is easily worked and is in very good heart, while in most seasons cultivations can be completed before cereal harvest begins. The only shortcomings of this succession is the danger that a residual infection of pea weevil may impair clover establishment.

Unfortunately, in Northumberland the cereal harvest is so late that there is insufficient time for reseeding after cereals, unless one follows the increasingly popular practice of sowing winter barley which usually can be harvested early in August Here we evolved a system of July–August reseeding after Italian ryegrass which has been established in a cereal crop in the previous year. This, in a sense, represents a compromise between two recognised methods of establishing pasture. As only 24 kg of Italian ryegrass are sown per hectare, there is relatively little at stake if the fully fertilised cereal crop lodges, or if there is mechanical damage from heavy equipment during a wet harvest. No clover is sown with the ryegrass so it is possible to adopt normal spraying for weeds if required.

Of course, this practice necessitates the use of nitrogenous fertilisers on the ryegrass to get full production from it. In most years an application of 40–55 kg per hectare of nitrogenous fertiliser immediately after harvest gives a good flush of stubble feed, which is especially valuable for wintering in-lamb ewes. A further dressing in the early spring will give feed that takes the burden off long-term leys which are allowed to retain leaf at a critical time of the year. Usually towards the end of April further nitrogen is applied, and the ryegrass is then closed for a silage cut which is taken at the beginning of June. Nearly two months intervene before reseeding, and this period can be used for a half-fallow to destroy couch grass and other weeds.

This approach to reseeding has been a very successful one from a farm management view-point, because we have an area for out-of-season grazing which we do not mind poaching because it is in a cheaply-established ley. Furthermore, both our summer-established long leys and the Italian are there to help us through the critical month of April, when all the mouths on the farm are hungry mouths. When the land is out of production in June, July and August, there is less grazing pressure on available pastures than there is at any time of the year, for by this time the silage and hay aftermaths are making their contribution.

PREPARATION OF LAND

Turning now to seedbeds, it is absolutely essential to create a really fine bed, which should also be a firm one. A fine seedbed promotes both an even distribution of seed and a more uniform depth of seeding. To ensure good germination and speedy establishment grass and clover seed should be sown at a depth of 12–20 mm. With seed at this level, seedling mortalities will be at a minimum, for the roots will get down to moisture even in dry conditions. Seeds which are on the surface, or which are barely covered will germinate if there is sufficient moisture in the soil, but they are very vulnerable should dry conditions follow germination – a circumstance not uncommon in April and May.

The certain placement of seed at the 12–20 mm level necessitates drilling rather than broadcasting, unless one adopts the safeguard of a heavy seeding rate to ensure that sufficient seed is at the optimum depth. The relatively new close-spaced drill is an ideal machine for drilling grass seeds. The costs are high but the recent development of contractor services for this purpose is very often the answer, and the saving in seed rate by using this service often more than compensates for the cost of the operation, as well as ensuring in most circumstances a better germination and take. Many farmers who practise drilling use a corn drill in a double operation on diagonals to increase the amount of ground cover and to reduce inter-seeding competition. At its best this is only a half-satisfactory expedient. Spread of seed is limited and there is a waste of time, machine and labour, which are resources that should be conserved in our farming.

The case for drilling is stronger with spring seeding, because of the danger of early-summer drought, than it is with the later summer establishment which, except perhaps in years of protracted summer drought, is usually succeeded by favourable soil moisture conditions.

When a grass seed drill is not available the last cultural operation before broadcasting should be with the Cambridge roller, and preferably with one of sufficient weight to leave deep grooves to gather the seed and secure optimum coverage. A light harrowing will follow to cover the seed, and finally a further heavy rolling will complete the seeding process. It is vital to get adequate consolidation at this point. Too often one sees the failure to consolidate properly reflected by the vigour or establishment where the tractor wheels have made their impression, and by indifferent establishment elsewhere in the field. This is particularly noticeable on headlands which have been adequately consolidated.

An extremely useful roller to effect the sort of consolidation needed is that illustrated by Plate 10a. It is home-made, consisting of three 900 mm diameter concrete pipes which are filled with concrete and are fitted with stub axles. Each roller of the gang of three is only 750 mm wide, so that it follows the contours and there is a minimum of bridging if the ground is a little uneven. The whole unit weighs 3 tonne and you can certainly see where it has been after the operation. It is especially valuable for summer reseeds, because not only does it shatter surface clods, but it gives a really firm finish – a vital factor in securing success for late-season establishment. It has a special value, too, on soils which carry flints or stones; because they are pressed down out of harm's way. Machinery manufacturers have also produced very useful plain rollers for this purpose either concrete or water ballasted. An added advantage of water ballast is that the weight can be varied to suit conditions.

UNDERSOWING OF PASTURES

There are two further problems to be discussed for the benefit of those who still elect to establish their pastures under a cereal crop. The first is the timing of seeding, and the second is the choice of cereal.

Our preference is to get grass seeds in as soon as possible after the corn has been drilled. Apart from any other consideration, the earlier that seeding is effected the greater are the chances of sound establishment as a safeguard against early summer drought. Secondly, especially if the land is in good heart, or if normal fertilising is adopted, seeding before germination of the cereal will minimise the effects of competition. Seeding into a well-established cereal crop will be successful only under favourable conditions, and these one cannot expect every year.

Farmers' preferences for a companion cereal vary over the

length and breadth of the country. In the south, the preference is for barley, because this is so often the last corn crop in the rotation. In addition it has the advantage of producing less straw to smother the seeds than either spring wheat or oats. Oats is a much more popular companion cereal in the north, primarily because it is often the last cereal in the rotation.

This consideration apart, barley is much to be preferred over spring oats. It has less straw, and it matures earlier, so that there is a better prospect of getting the field cleared in time to allow for a maximum of autumn growth. Spring wheat on the other hand, is invariably the last cereal to be harvested, although the modern varieties have excellent standing qualities.

COMPANION PLANTS IN DIRECT ESTABLISHMENTS

Turning now to direct reseeding, it is generally advantageous to sow pasture seeds with a companion grazing nurse crop, which may be a cereal, or a light seeding of rape or soft turnips, or a combination of both. Our preference is for a cereal rather than rape, except perhaps on upland reseeds. Under favourable conditions the rape may grow too strongly even at low seeds rates of 1–2 kg per hectare and because grazing must be delayed for the sake of the stock until the rape is 'ripe' there is a danger of smothering the seeds.

Oats and wheat, being the more palatable, are preferable to barley if a cereal is used as a cover but usually the choice is determined by what is available. In most years there is some surplus treated cereal seed and the use of it as a grazing nurse crop is a convenient and gainful means of disposal. A seeding of 70–90 kg of cereal per hectare is ample for this purpose.

There are two major reasons for including a grazing nurse crop when direct establishment is undertaken. First it results in a greater production of herbage, and secondly it is helpful in controlling competition from annual weeds. Grass, as well as clover seeds, are slow in making a showing in the spring, and especially is this true with slow-establishing species like timothy and meadow fescue. The cereal will make good growth within a month from seeding, to provide feed for stock at a time when weeds are in an early seedling stage and are relatively palatable.

Apart from grazing, trampling also has a deterrent effect upon weeds at this stage, and weed control apart, one cannot overstress the importance of getting stock on to pasture as quickly as possible. Most Kent farmers believe that stock, preferably sheep, should be put on a pasture as soon as there is a reasonable blush of green showing. This belief stems from a recognition of the importance both of consolidation and of the value of fertility from excrements. Stapledon always stressed this feature of the golden hoof in pasture establishment.

When stocking pastures at this stage the best course is to put a lot of stock on for a short time, thus effecting a quick grazing, and then to rest the pasture until grazing is again justified. Above all, it is important to keep on top of the pasture in these early stages to ensure that there is adequate light for the development of clovers.

FERTILITY REQUIREMENTS

Mention of fertility leads us to a consideration of fertiliser requirements in grass sward establishment. Here one cannot generalise, but surely one cannot expect a fully-productive pasture if the land is acid, or if there is a deficiency of phosphate and potash. Where these are necessary, they should be worked into the soil immediately before seeding so that there is plant food within the root range of the developing seedlings.

Opinions differ as to the amount of nitrogenous fertiliser to be used in the seedbed. Certainly some added nitrogen is usually essential, especially if the reseed follows a cereal or Italian ryegrass, when soil nitrogen will be depleted. A total of

35–50 kg nitrogen per hectare will be adequate to get the grasses moving. Even at this moderate level, care must be taken to ensure that clovers are not swamped by the growth of grass, by appropriate hard grazing.

When pastures are undersown in cereals intended for harvest it may be advisable, for the sake of the seeds, to broadcast the fertiliser rather than apply it to the cereal with the combine drill. If this is done, it is important to remember that broadcasting of fertiliser is only about half as effective as placement so far as the cereal is concerned. In other words, 500 kg of complete fertiliser which is broadcast has about the same effect as 250 kg down the spout. The combining of fertiliser may be preferred on land where there is a danger of the seeds 'growing up through the band', but this is not a likely happening if the cereal is sown early at a normal seed rate.

MANAGEMENT AFTER ESTABLISHMENT

Management of undersown seeds after harvest should be directed towards the building up of root reserves before onset of winter. Avoidance of continuous grazing is preferred and it is wise to stock heavily for short periods alternated by longer periods of rest. Usually two grazings, with the second after the onset of hard frost, will be ample for these maiden seeds.

In their first spring it is preferable to use maiden seeds for grazing rather than for conservation. Here again it is a question of giving the clover a chance to develop, and to ensure that there is a build-up of fertility from stock droppings. This advice runs counter to usual practice in the north of Britain, where it is common to include some Italian ryegrass and red clover in the ley mixture in order to take a heavy hay crop in the first harvest year. On balance, it is better farming practice to graze a ley in its first season rather than take hay from it. If conservation is essential, then it is preferable to take an early cut of silage, if the pasture is to be fully productive.

ARABLE SILAGE AS A NURSE CROP

Finally, a word about using arable silage as a nurse crop for pasture establishment. The system is a useful one in that cover is removed relatively early in the growing season and there is enough time for the pasture plants to tiller out and make a sole. Our biggest objection to the method is based upon a dislike of arable silage as a feedingstuff.

Even when made under ideal conditions, there is not much milk or meat in it compared with pasture silage. Made under bad conditions, where there is soiling of the herbage, there is a considerable loss of palatability, and a depression of digestibility. Usually arable silage can be regarded as little better than a maintenance food, and its greatest virtue is that of a heavy crop. This means that, when it is removed, there is a severe depletion of fertility, and usually it will be necessary to apply about 400 kg of complete fertiliser to make good this loss and give a boost to pasture establishment.

Chapter 13

MANURING OF GRASSLAND

Already, in fairly general terms, emphasis has been given to the necessity for adequate soil fertility if the more productive species are to persist and give of their best. It now remains to give a more precise account of fertiliser practices. Before this can be done, however, it is necessary to debate the general economics of applying fertilisers to grassland.

Unfortunately it is impossible to give a satisfactory answer to someone who asks for advice on fertiliser practice without a very intimate knowledge, not only of the farm, but of the farmer's efficiency in using the grass he grows. Here we are up against the problem that, unlike a cash crop, grass does not generally become money until it is turned into milk or meat.

That indefinable personal factor which determines quality of management, together with variations in climate and soil, makes it impossible to give advice with any precision. One can confidently recommend farmers at the top end of the scale, especially those engaged in dairying, to use up to 350 kg N per hectare, in addition to basic dressings of lime, phosphate and potash where these are necessary, because they are capable of getting a good return on their investment. At the other end of the scale, with less intensive pastoral production, there are those who could be well advised to limit their inputs to periodic liming and slagging when soil analysis suggest that these are advisable. For reasons already outlined dairy pastures will invariably support higher fertiliser inputs than those grazed by sheep or beef cattle.

There is, however, a complication in the economics of fertilising dairy pastures in the shape of levels of concentrate usage. A dairy farmer is able to share his returns with both the provender and fertiliser trades and make a good living, up to a certain point. Beyond this he will lose out unless his stock and his stockmanship are of such a standard that he is able to get very high yields. If he is getting only average yields, both per cow and per hectare, there is a very real danger that food costs per litre will be prohibitively high.

The implication is that a farmer who spends a lot of money on fertilising his grassland must intensify his stocking rate to ensure full utilisation, and this may mean lower yields per cow. At the same time, he must make every effort to ensure that the grass he offers his herd, whether it be grazing or in a conserved form, is of the highest quality. This latter provision will make for economies in the use of concentrates, either by feeding less per cow or by reducing the level of protein in the concentrate mixture. Whenever one examines the accounts of those dairy farmers who are making high profits out of intensive grassland farming, invariably they have a much higher concentration of stock and a much lower expenditure per litre on concentrates than are found on the average farm.

GENERAL PRINCIPLES

Regarding the type of farming, the starting point in designing a fertilising programme is an up-to-date soil analysis which gives details of the phosphate, potash and lime status of the farm and it is wise to have the soils of a farm re-tested at least every 4–5 years. Even farmers who feel that they have been reasonably generous in their manuring, may find no improvement, and sometimes a decline, in the fertility status of some fields, despite their generosity. This is especially true on farms practising alternate husbandry.

There was a time when home mixing of fertilisers was a regular feature of farming and a useful wet weather job. However, with the greater pressure on farm labour and the wide range of formulations of granulated fertilisers that are now available to suit most needs, home mixing is a forgotten chore. This does not mean that straight fertilisers are no longer important but normally they will be applied separately to meet a precise requirement. For instance phosphate needs can be satisfactorily met more economically by periodic application of superphosphate or triple superphosphate. A single dressing of muriate of potash will cater for any potassium deficiency while nitrogen, applied in several doses over the course of the year, will now usually take the form of ammonium nitrate.

There is much to be said for applying straights rather than compounds to grassland now that most fertilisers are granulated and can be spread very satisfactorily by spinners which are cheap tools with a very high output. Again in the present state of knowledge, it appears to be unwise to apply potash to pastures in the early spring for at this time of the year, especially when associated with liberal nitrogen dressings, there is a luxury uptake of potassium which is at the expense of magnesium. There are grounds for believing that this will precipitate hypomagnesaemia, perhaps better known to farmers as grass staggers, which is particularly a hazard with lactating animals.

The safest time to apply a heavy dressing of potash to grazing pastures is in June–July when clover is making its maximum contribution, for it has a higher magnesium content than the grass component of the sward. Where it is intended to conserve grass either as hay or silage an early spring application of potash and nitrogen in combination seems to be quite safe.

Once this need has been satisfied and, assuming that there are ample potash reserves in the soil, further manuring can be limited to straight nitrogen applications at appropriate times of the year. If potash is seriously deficient this may necessitate a dressing with straight muriate of potash. Alternatively, if the potash deficiency is only moderate and fertilising also involves the use of nitrogen, then a nitrogen-potash compound can be applied. Where nitrogen is not required, the use of such a compound would be a needlessly expensive way of making good potash deficiency.

Potash is seldom a limiting factor to pasture growth on clay soils, as it is commonly on light soils such as chalks and gravels especially if a high nitrogen policy is combined with a heavy conservation programme, for instance, two or three cuts for silage in the one season. Twenty tonnes of leafy grass – the yield from a hectare of reasonably good grass just at the point of ear emergence contains the equivalent potassium of 125 kg of muriate of potash, so inevitably successive crops for conservation will rapidly deplete the potassium reserves in a soil. Whereas an application of the order of 70 kg of K_2O per hectare will suffice for the grazing block of a two-sward system under a high nitrogen regime, the cutting block will require up to four times this amount of K_2O. A mid summer application of an NPK compound will often suffice on the grazing block, but it is recommended, on grounds of being more economical, to apply straight potash to the conservation block which incidentally should be the principal destination of slurry which, applied in the winter, can be a useful source of both potash and phosphate for the following conservation crops.

TIMING OF APPLICATIONS

The timing of phosphate applications does not appear to be particularly important under British conditions. Timing of nitrogen dressings is a much more critical matter, especially in respect of applications for early-bite grazing. Here the advice is to stagger the nitrogen top-dressing programme, partly to ensure a succession of growth to meet grazing needs, but mainly to reduce losses by leaching during unfavourable weather conditions in the early spring.

When it comes to back-end nitrogenous dressings, the later one goes into September the less likelihood there is of a worthwhile response, although farmers in the more favoured districts have more latitude in this respect. One is entitled to take a risk, however, if grass supplies are short as a result of summer drought, as they were in the autumn of 1976. In this year, applied nitrogen did not show any appreciable effect till early October, when there was sufficient soil moisture. The ground was then still warm enough for nitrogen to give a worthwhile response, and this was particularly true of Italian ryegrass stands.

The colder and wetter the summer, the more important it is to get nitrogen on early for the autumn flush. In the north-east, we had greater confidence in making this final dressing of nitrogen in August, but it still appears to be worthwhile to apply it to undersown Italian as the stubbles are cleared during the first ten days of September.

NITROGEN FERTILISING PRACTICE

Ammonium nitrate in the form of prills, due to its cheaper cost per unit than other forms, has taken over a very large proportion of the market. It must be remembered that it has no soil neutralising power and with continuous heavy use can induce soil acidity which must be corrected by the use of lime. Another virtue is its concentration as compared with nitro chalk and this reduces the handling burden.

The whole question of the conflict between bag and clover nitrogen was debated in an earlier chapter, and it was pointed out that at intermediate levels of dressing there was a likelihood of falling between two stools. This is illustrated by the following table based on a study undertaken some years ago in Northern Ireland where research workers have been particularly interested in the relative contributions of clover and fertiliser nitrogen.

At levels of 250, 500 and even 1,000 kg of nitro chalk per

Average annual yields of dry matter from a reseeded pasture receiving adequate lime, phosphate and potash (kg per hectare)

Applied Nitrogen	Grass	Clover	Total	Response kg Nitrogen
0 nitro-chalk	4,769	3,891	8,660	—
250 ,,	5,899	2,912	8,811	1·0
500 ,,	6,777	2,385	9,162	1·0
1,000 ,,	8,911	1,004	9,915	1·25
1,500 ,,	10,542	251	10,793	1·42
2,500 ,,	12,801	126	12,937	1·70

hectare the response per kg in terms of dry matter was much smaller than it was at 1,500 or 2,500 kg. This is explained by the appreciable decline in the clover fraction which occurred even when only 250 kg of nitro chalk were applied annually. It seems that the applied nitro chalk was doing little more at the 250 and 500 kg level than make good the reduction of clover nitrogen it effected. It is noteworthy, however, that nitro chalk applied at a rate as high as 2,500 kg per hectare was 70 per cent more effective per kg than it was at 500 kg per hectare. One sees in these figures the danger of adopting a compromise between the two extremes of fertiliser practice over a whole farm.

In adopting a heavy nitrogen programme, there is no point in applying this fertiliser regardless of the availability of grass, whether it is for stock or for conservation. There must be a very high measure of opportunism in using nitrogenous fertilisers. If there is a pressure on available grass, then immediate applications will be justified, at least on part of the grassland, but if grass supplies are adequate then the fertiliser is best kept in the store. This may also be true during drought periods when water, not nitrogen, is limiting growth. Fertiliser nitrogen must be a sensibly used tool and not an addiction in intensive grassland management, although the problem is to predict climatic conditions in good time and apply the appropriate quantity to maintain a steady supply for stock.

MINOR ELEMENTS

The major elements in plant nutrition, nitrogen, phosphate
and potassium, along with calcium to counter soil acidity, were
the only concern of grassland farmers until the early thirties.
Since then research both in Britain and abroad, thanks to new
techniques of micro-analysis, established the importance of
minor elements, not only for normal plant growth but also for
the well-being of animals. In the latter instance possibly the
best known deficiency is that of cobalt, which is required in
very minute quantities to ensure normal thrift. One part per
million of cobalt in the dry matter of herbage can mean the
difference between normal condition as opposed to a wasting
death in ruminants grazing what appears to be a first class
pasture. In Britain the condition, well recognised in sheep in
certain localities, is known as 'pine' and in New Zealand as
'bush sickness'. In the latter country it was first diagnosed as
iron deficiency and protection was given to stock by providing
access to mineral mixtures containing limonite, provided the
limonite came from one particular source. Subsequently it was
established that this particular limonite contained an appreciable amount of cobalt.

It was two Australian scientists, Filmer and Underwood,
who cracked the cobalt nut about 1935 in their investigations of
a similar wasting disease in southern Australia. The good news
spread quickly and a deficiency of cobalt was soon established
as the culprit responsible for a number of wasting diseases in
several parts of the world. Attention was also focused on other
trace elements and more deficiency diseases were recognised,
in particular copper deficiency leading to a condition known
in New Zealand as peat scours which occurs on soils reclaimed
from peat swamps. Copper deficiency can also be a problem in
Britain. The best known example is possibly swayback in
lambs which is associated with a low copper content of
herbage, especially in an open spring on reclaimed marginal

land. Copper deficiency can also affect young cattle in Britain and with black animals there is a tell-tale dilution of the pigment in the hair to give a distinct bronzing.

A third mineral deficiency which has been recognised comparatively recently is one of selenium which is associated with muscular dystrophy. Only very minute quantities of selenium are required for normal health and its importance was only recognised when highly sophisticated methods of micro-analysis became available.

Grassland farmers in the southern hemisphere, with characteristic concern for labour economy, favour the application of fertilisers containing a salt of the deficient element, e.g. copperised or cobaltised superphosphate, rather than more direct treatment of animals which is the method favoured in Britain, e.g. by the provision of mineral supplements, dosing, or injections.

Apart from animal diseases arising from deficiencies of trace elements there are deficiencies affecting plant growth but unlike cobalt or copper they have no deleterious effect on the grazing animal.

One of the most notable of these is sulphur and there are parts of the world where the response to superphosphate, once attributed to its phosphate content, is now recognised as being due in part at least to its sulphur. We are unlikely to encounter this situation in Britain where industrial fouling of the atmosphere includes considerable quantities of sulphur dioxide which probably does more harm than good to plant growth in highly industrialised areas such as parts of West Yorkshire.

Molybdenum, again in very minute quantities, is essential for the normal growth of legumes. Apparently it is required for the proper development of the associated nitrogen-fixing bacteria. With a deficiency of molybdenum there is a poor establishment of clover and an almost complete absence of nodulation. The quantity of molybdenum required for normal growth is unbelievably minute but, in excess of as little as

20 parts per million in the dry matter of pasture, it is associated with a condition known as teart poisoning, characteristic of parts of Somerset and Gloucestershire. The apparent effect of the high molybdenum is on the retention and utilisation of copper. No response to molybdenum has been established in Britain and this is possibly very fortunate because of the risk that over-generous applications in an attempt to rectify deficiencies could do more harm than good.

Other deficiencies of minor elements have been established, for instance manganese and boron, but their impact and their prevention have been a concern of arable rather than grassland farmers in Britain. This does not mean that they are potentially unimportant in maximising production from pasture, especially in soils with a high pH for this may limit the uptake of some essential minor elements. There have been instances of boron deficiency affecting the establishment of lucerne and it is possible that other legumes may also be affected on this account.

Chapter 14

IMPROVEMENT OF PERMANENT PASTURES AND ROUGH GRAZINGS

The virtues of good permanent pastures have been extolled, but this must in no sense be interpreted as an open testimonial, applicable to all permanent pastures. To the contrary, for the overwhelming proportion of them leave a great deal to be desired. In many cases the circumstances are such that they should be ploughed at the first convenient opportunity, so that a fresh start may be made to provide a basis of more desirable species, or else to create a surface that permits mowing as part of their management. In other cases there will be a sufficient foundation on which to build, using surface improvement techniques only.

Sometimes some surface improvement must be undertaken before it is advisable to plough. The most important pasture group falling into this category mainly consists of upland grazings, where there is a layer of peat with a cover of low-producing acid-tolerant grasses, rushes, and possibly heather. If this layer is ploughed in it may remain undecomposed at ploughing depth for many years to impede drainage, prevent root penetration, and create ideal conditions for rush invasion. The correct approach to reclamation on such land is to break down this top layer by surface improvement methods before ploughing is attempted, if ploughing has to be used at all.

Drainage usually has to be undertaken as a first operation because normally such soils are poorly drained. This will be followed by the application of lime and phosphates and, above all, by the concentration of stock to eat out dominant species and to effect hoof cultivation which assist in breaking the surface mat. More breeding cows on the Welsh hills for example could result in a rapid acceleration of improvement of swards based on *Molinia* and *Nardus* with some fescue present.

USE OF STOCK

Here one is thinking of stock as tools in pasture management. Nowhere has this function been illustrated to better effect in recent years than in New Zealand, where 'mob-stocking' following aerial top dressing with phosphate has transformed inferior store stock pastures on steep unploughable land to a point where they are now capable of producing fat lambs. Mob-stocking implies the concentration of a large number of stock on a limited area for relatively short periods of time.

Short periods are stressed because stock which are made to work for a living in this way cannot be punished too severely, and it will generally be necessary to give them some relief from their labours. This necessitates subdivision of the area to be reclaimed, at least down to the field unit size which will ultimately be adopted on the farm.

Ewes or single-suckling cows after weaning can be used for this purpose, but their availability is limited to a relatively short period. The ideal time to hit *Molinia,* a characteristic grass of such areas, is in the early summer period when it is starting to make growth and has some semblance of palatability. In-calf heifers, up to two or three months before they are due to calve, are admirable for this work, but one has to use considerable judgment in handling stock in this way, so that harm is not done to them, and one must be prepared to provide good feed later to compensate for any set-back in condition. One of the arguments supporting August calving of suckler cows on upland farms is that with April weaning there are two critical months, May and June, when the dry cows are available to work for a living without detriment to their own subsequent performance and, in the process, do much good for the balance of species.

The best approach is to have three or four enclosures that are being improved at the one time, so that some form of rotational grazing can be practised. This will be good for the stock and also for the work in hand.

SURFACE SEEDING

Provided land is reasonably dry and there is some natural shelter, good work will be done during the late autumn and early winter by cattle receiving supplementary feeding which includes fairly mature hay, because this results in a considerable measure of seeding. Another device for introducing clover to such areas is to lay up an already improved area of the farm in the summer to allow clover seed heads to mature. If these are eaten by sheep which are shifted from this grazing to the areas under improvement a number of times, there is a very appreciable seeding of clover which will become effective if phosphate and lime have been applied in sufficient quantities to allow the clover to establish.

There is also the more straightforward but rather more expensive approach of broadcasting grass and clover seed on a surface that has been cleared with hard grazing and burning following the use of a desiccant such as paraquat, possibly with light rotovation where this is possible and using sheep to tread in the seed. Under some circumstances, harrowing in of seed can be very effective. Surface seeding in this way has been effectively practised in parts of Scotland on thin soils where outcrops or boulders prevent normal cultivation. Initial progress by such methods may seem slow, but usually there is an acceleration once the process gets under way and soil conditions start to improve.

Someone with plenty of capital who is on cultivatable land will usually prefer speedier methods, such as pioneer cropping followed by direct reseeding. But the farmer with limited capital, both for land improvement and for stocking pastures once they have been improved, will find that this gradual approach will suit him very well. He can raise his sheep and cattle numbers by a process of natural increase rather than by purchase, and in this way he maintains his farm in equilibrium.

Too often one encounters examples where men have used most of their available capital in large-scale improvement schemes and have insufficient livestock to exploit these improvements. If improved pastures are not stocked adequately, they will soon deteriorate as a consequence of invasion by the less desirable species that are encouraged by under-grazing.

When dealing with marginal land with only limited capital it is usually advisable to work to a long-term plan, with ploughing and reseeding playing only a limited part on those areas which are ready for this more expensive method of land rehabilitation.

The more recently developed technique of chemical ploughing, using one of the new materials which destroy grass is potentially a valuable aid to the improvement of such land. Once the herbage has been killed a match can be put to it on a dry day without too much wind, and trash will burn to leave a reasonably clear surface for scratching with harrows and over-sowing with grass and clover seeds or by the use of the numerous sod-seeding machines now available provided the land is tractable. Once established, however, good management is particularly essential to prevent deterioration by invasion of rushes. It must be stressed, however, that marginal land farming cannot afford expensive inputs, because usually the occupier has to make his living at the same time as he improves his farm.

LOWLAND PASTURES

When one comes to more tractable land at lower altitudes, problems of permanent pasture improvement are not nearly so difficult. In fact, on a great deal of this land, though grasses like

Agrostis may dominate, there are often already appreciable proportions of the more desirable species such as ryegrass, timothy and white clover which can be encouraged if the fertility level of the soil is raised and intensive grazing is practised.

Anyone who saw the Treefield experiment at Cockle Park before it was ploughed out will appreciate the importance of these factors in transforming derelict permanent grass. Plot 6, the control, continued for sixty years as a low producing association of bent grasses and fine-leaved fescues with scarcely a trace of wild white clover. The adjacent plots, which received 625 kg of slag per hectare at three-yearly intervals to make good the principal deficiency which was phosphate, had approximately five times the productivity of the control. The process of improvement is a cumulative one, for with the increase in clover due to slagging, increased stocking is possible. This, in turn, through the larger returns of excrements, raises the fertility status to the point where productive species like perennial ryegrass are dominant in the sward.

It is not enough to apply fertilisers. One must also create the other biotic conditions which will favour the spread of productive species and which will discourage weeds – for example, drainage where this is necessary. It is also very important to let light into the sward, for both ryegrass and white clover require light as well as fertility if they are to tiller freely. A grassland reclamation exercise initiated a number of years ago by a farmer with inherently fertile marshland near Winchelsea in East Sussex illustrates the importance of this factor in a dramatic way. He was also an orchardist on adjacent land and he was in the fortunate situation of having a gang mower which played a key part in the initial years of reclamation. The first step was the very necessary one of lowering the water table by cleaning out dykes and by effecting general improvements in drainage. The second was the repeated use of the gang mower in association with intensive grazing.

Formerly the pasture contained a large amount of rough grass interspersed with horsetail, rushes and thistles, and it provided nothing more than some summer keep for store stock. Today it is a dense mat, predominantly ryegrass and white clover, and it can be classed among the most productive pastures in this country, regularly producing well over 600 kg of liveweight increase per hectare.

Not many farmers have gang mowers, or indeed surfaces which will carry them, but they have other tools which will do the same sort of job – namely their grazing animals, mowing machines and forage harvesters. One way of dealing with a rough type of permanent pasture which carried dead growth is to give it a fairly good application of nitrogen, say 60 kg N per hectare, in addition to its basic fertiliser needs, and to take a silage crop which is cut before the crop gets yellow in the bottom. There will be clean, fresh growth in the aftermath, and because nearly all the rough growth has been removed there will be a chance for the clover to run during the summer, provided the aftermath is not permitted to grow too strongly. Here again, a programme of heavy stocking for short periods followed by rests is ideal to promote this advantage for white clover.

CONTROL OF WEEDS

Sometimes the preliminary step must be taken of reducing weed population before such fertilising, cutting and grazing management can be exploited to full advantage. The most serious weeds of old grassland are daisies, buttercups, thistles (especially creeping thistles) rushes and docks.

Improvements in drainage and fertility levels are in themselves methods of reducing the incidence of some of these weeds, especially buttercups and rushes. One of the most spectacular features of the Hanging Leaves experiment at Cockle Park was the virtual absence of rushes on the drained area of the field. On the undrained portion there were relatively few rushes where slag was applied, but where slag was omitted rushes were the dominant vegetation.

Today hormone weed killers can be utilised to advantage in controlling many weeds in grassland and considerable success has been achieved in handling rushes in this way. MCPA is commonly used, although it is likely that this herbicide will impair clover growth if this species is present. Less harm will be done if the chemical is applied fairly early in the spring, before clover starts to grow actively. However, if clover is already very deficient, it may be advisable to ignore its welfare in the first instance and make a job of clearing the weeds, depending on subsequent surface seeding with clover to make good this deficiency.

Rushes, of course, will not stand repeated mowing, but on much land carrying a dense plant of rushes, mowing is out of the question until they have been severely reduced by spraying and drainage. Even then it may be necessary to plough and level, in order to get a reasonable mowing surface.

Mowing is also one of the most effective methods of dealing with thistles, whether they be in permanent pasture or leys. Mowing is less effective if it is just a matter of topping, because the rosette form taken by thistles under grazing conditions helps them to survive cutting. If, however, the pasture is allowed to grow to the silage stage twice in the one season and the thistles are cut when they are in full growth, there will be very few remaining in the following year.

Docks are a more difficult problem, especially on dairy pastures where fertility is high, but they are much more of a menace in ley farming than in well-managed permanent pasture. The aim must be to prevent them setting seed, and here silage making is infinitely preferable to hay making, especially when hay is cut at a very mature stage. Mature hay, carrying ripe dock seeds, is an abomination, because it is probably the main agent in spreading the dock nuisance.

Docks were becoming an increasing weed menace up to the

introduction of specialist dock sprays a few years ago which, although expensive, are reasonably effective. Hard grazing with sheep is almost as effective as any other method of dealing with docks. It is also an excellent way of controlling ragwort because sheep will eat out the crown of this noxious weed to prevent seeding and further spreading.

SOD SEEDING

Sod seeding is now a practicable proposition on permanent pastures on the better soils where there are no problems of destroying a surface mat or rough vegetation. In Australia, New Zealand and North America, sod seeding is well past the experimental stage and is now part of farm practice. A common New Zealand method is to fit special cutting tips to a drill which has hoe-type coulters. These rip the turf and expose sufficient soil to allow the seeds to strike. Where there are no stones, a disc coulter drill can be very useful, if it is used when the soil is fairly moist. This not only results in a more effective cut, but it gives the seeds a better chance of germinating. As mentioned earlier some types are based on modified strengthened Suffolk-type coulter drills or disc drills, and others are based on the rotary cultivator.

If conditions allow, rolling should follow the seeding. If this is not possible, then mob-stocking should be substituted, not just immediately after seeding, but at frequent intervals thereafter to reduce competition and over-shadowing by the originally established species.

There are two periods of the year when sod seeding can be attempted – either in the spring or in the late summer, i.e. the July–August period in Britain. At either time the pasture should be eaten bare, even to the point of being 'poached red' as our Irish friends would say. Spring seeding will possibly give a better prospect of clover establishment, but here again it is a question of ensuring that there is no smothering of seedlings, by appropriate grazing. Perennial ryegrass, which is very quick to establish, especially with summer seedings when the ground is warm, is the most certain grass to sow. In New Zealand there have been impressive results with *Grasslands Manawa* ryegrass, and over-sowing has now become a standard method of introducing this valuable out-of-season producer into a permanent grass system without recourse to the plough.

Seed rates of 12 kg per hectare of ryegrass and 2 kg of white clover per hectare appear to be ample when the seed is drilled in, but somewhat higher seed rates will be necessary, say 18 kg in all, if broadcasting following some discing and harrowing is done on a bared pasture. We used this last method quite successfully at Cockle Park in a wet July–August period when there was ample moisture to promote germination and seedling survival. A double cut with the discs exposed enough soil to get a take, and this was safeguarded by heavy rolling immediately after seeding. A modified system used by the junior author at the Welsh Agricultural College has been rotary cultivation at a depth of 5–7 cm on old grassland using the special tines provided by the manufacturers to break the pan so often formed by rotary cultivators. This has resulted in a system where stiff yellow clay some 10–12 cm below the surface is not brought up and is often helpful in a dry autumn, as there is less moisture loss than there is with ploughing.

IMPORTANCE OF MANAGEMENT

Once a permanent pasture has been brought into reasonable shape, it is important that it is not allowed to backslide to its former state of semi-productivity. Avoid over-grazing in the spring when there is a danger of poaching, for invariably this will encourage weeds like buttercups and daisies, especially on strong land. Later in the season it is equally important to avoid the twin evil of under-grazing, for this will give rise to neglected clumps of rough herbage which will weaken the clover and encourage poorer species like *Poa trivialis* and Yorkshire fog.

Repeated cutting for hay, especially at an advanced stage of growth, has a similar deleterious effect. Apart from the danger of depleting fertility, tall growing species come into an ascendancy at the expense of ryegrass and white clover, which must be regarded as a climax association in a permanent pasture. Occasional cutting, however, especially at the early silage stage, is sound practice, for it removes the clumps that will be neglected by stock before they cause harm.

Above all, there should be no fear of eating a permanent pasture bare in the late summer immediately prior to the onset of the autumn flush. Not only will this give a better quality of back-end grazing, but it will help pasture composition. A permanent pasture should not be put up for a strong growth of foggage year after year, however, because this will lead to cocksfoot and Yorkshire fog becoming dominant in the sward.

Finally, the precaution of obtaining soil analyses at regular intervals is stressed, so that the all-important consideration of plant nutrient status is safeguarded. The starting point for a good pasture and the maintenance of its quality is a fertile soil, preferably with a pH of about 6·5 and adequate levels of phosphate and potash. Good management in other respects such as avoidance of poaching and under- or over-grazing will only succeed on a foundation of basic fertility.

Chapter 15

CONSERVATION OF GRASS

Any method of conservation of grass – as hay, silage and to a lesser extent as dried grass – entails waste, in that the final product fed to stock invariably has a lower feeding value than the grass when standing in the field. A striking example of this is silage. Although cut in mid-May, when one would expect a dairy cow to maintain herself and produce 18–24 litres of milk per day, it ends up as a product that even under the best conditions of maintaining a cow with sufficient energy for 9 litres of milk and enough protein for 18 litres. Under poor conditions, with an indifferent fermentation and surface waste, this difference between the raw material and the finished product may well be more. Haymaking can show greater losses still, up to a point of total loss when a crop rain-soaked for some 3–4 weeks may have to be disposed of by setting fire to it.

The safest method of preserving the feeding value of the herbage at point of cutting and, in the process, minimising conservation losses, is by artificial drying, but thanks to the high costs of fossil energy this is no longer a proposition for the ordinary farmer. Virtually the only outlet for dried grass (or lucerne) is as a source of carotene for food mixes.

GROWTH IN POPULARITY OF SILAGE

The ensiling of herbage is a process of considerable antiquity for it was practised by the early Egyptians and later by the Romans, but it is only comparatively recently that it has had a well-defined place in British farming. Some silage was made in the latter half of the nineteenth century, while wooden tower silos were a very occasional feature of farmyards in the period between the wars when ICI attempted without much success to popularise the process. Among other things at Jeallot's Hill they experimented with the AIV process which had been pioneered in Finland. It involves the adding of dilute mineral acids to the green material at the point of ensiling to lower pH and prevent butyric fermentation. Needless to say with dairy concentrates as cheap and as freely available as they were in the thirties, silage making in any form made no appreciable progress in Britain.

However the situation changed dramatically with the outbreak of war in 1939 and a drive to popularise silage was initiated by the Ministry of Agriculture and its agencies which continued throughout the forties. It made relatively little progress and farmers became very adept at advancing good reasons for not making the stuff. In retrospect this is not surprising for there was so much heavy manual labour in getting material into and out of stacks or improvised bunkers and with the great majority of dairy cows being housed in byres there was a considerable double handling of what was too often a foul-smelling material that tainted exposed milk and permeated workers' clothes. This last feature made silage very unpopular with farm wives.

Gradually the arguments based on the heavy labour input of silage as compared with hay have been whittled away and the position has now been reached on many farms where there is less labour required in making and feeding silage than is needed for hay. The first major step in this direction was made by Rex Paterson in Hampshire about 1950 when he developed the buckrake and soon after this successfully introduced the concept of self-feeding silage by giving stock controlled access to a face of silage. The buckrake was soon followed by relatively cheap and efficient forage harvesters and with the availability of farm improvement grants more and more farmers, particularly dairymen, were able to erect in-wintering accommodation that was designed specifically with either self-feeding or easy feeding of silage, commonly made in covered clamps, as the basis of winter fodder provision. Through the fifties and sixties haymaking continued to be the dominant means of creating winter reserves. However, there was a growing feeling that silage was the more sensible product because of the fickleness of British weather and by 1980, in terms of conserved dry matter, silage was just as popular as hay. '

Another factor promoting its popularity was the growing confidence of farmers in the feeding value of silage if well made and the certainty of achieving such a product provided certain basic principles are observed. Unquestionably the so-called experts that promoted silage in the early days of the wartime drive gave a lot of erroneous advice and made the whole process unduly complicated. A thermometer was considered to be an essential tool because of a belief that the temperature of the mass had to rise to 45°C before more material was added, to reduce the risk of a butyric fermentation. The result too often was a chocolate-brown product, often quite palatable but with virtually no protein-sparing function. There was good cause to be concerned about the dangers of a secondary butyric fermentation, which is responsible for the foul odour that fortunately is now suffered less frequently than was once the case. This was due in the large to a widespread belief that silage could be made in any weather. This is quite erroneous, for ideally ensiled material should not carry any free moisture. Indeed there are strong arguments for ensiling wilted material which will be discussed later.

There was also a widely held view that there is some magic in the ensilage process that produces silk purses out of sow's ears. The senior author remembers an encounter in 1947 with a former university lecturer in agriculture, turned farmer, who had written what was then considered an authoritative pamphlet on silage. He was in the process of making silage with the first cut from a new stand of lucerne that was dominated by fat hen. He was surprised and hurt with the comment that it would be much less bother in the long run to put the rubbish directly on to the muck midden.

COMPARATIVE VALUE OF SILAGE

The simple truth is that silage is never any better, and very often much poorer, in feeding value than the original material put into the silo. In fact, with herbage cut at the same stage of growth and made into silage or hay, the probability is that hay made without weather damage and a consequent loss of leaf and palatability will have the higher nutritional value. This is illustrated by the following American figures* derived from *ad lib* feeding of three kinds of conserved food from the same crop to 300 kg heifers:

Food	Dry matter	Dry-matter intake per 100 kg body weight	Average daily liveweight gain
Unwilted silage	17·9%	1·60 kg	0·04 kg
Wilted silage	25·0%	2·01 kg	0·58 kg
Hay	84·1%	2·33 kg	0·76 kg

These figures stress the importance of a high dry-matter content in influencing the intake of dry matter by cattle and, in turn, the rate of liveweight gain. Similar experiments have been undertaken in the feeding of dairy cows, and here again one gets corresponding differences in dry-matter intake, though less marked differences in levels of milk production. It almost seems that silage dry-matter is converted more efficiently into milk than hay dry-matter from the same crop, but this does not appear to apply to liveweight gains.

The case for silage as opposed to hay does not rest, therefore on any superiority of silage as a feedingstuff, provided both are made from the same sort of material under ideal conditions. This last qualification is the rub in Britain,

* Everett, Lassiter, Huffman and Duncan, *Journal of Dairy Science*, 1958, p. 720.

PLATE 13a

The production of weaners from single-suckled cows is not sufficiently intensive to provide a good living for any but large-scale farmers who have relatively cheap land.

PLATE 13b

The dairy herd coming up the race for afternoon milking on Mr Charles Platt's Woore Hall Farm, Woore, Salop.

ICI Photo.

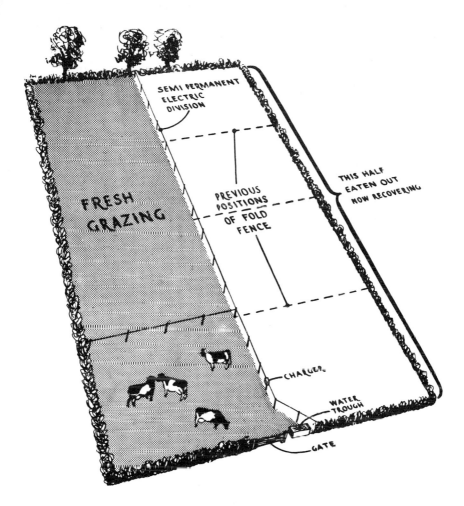

FIG. 1

Layout for fold grazing to protect recovery growth and to minimise labour in daily shifting of fold wires.

because it is so seldom that we have sufficient good weather to make really first-class hay. Although we usually have our best haymaking weather in late May and early June when pasture is at the appropriate stage of growth to make a really good product, the herbage is invariably so full of sap that drying is prolonged and the danger of weather damage is aggravated.

Quick haymaking methods and barn drying, which will be discussed later, may bring about greater certainty of saving early-cut hay in a reasonably good condition. For the present, however, the policy of the great majority of farmers is one of leaving hay to an advanced stage of growth, partly because this will mean quicker drying and partly because it will mean more bulk. In practice, therefore, the debate is on the relative merits of silage cut early in the season and hay cut at an advanced stage of growth.

Provided a farmer is equipped to make and feed silage economically, the arguments seem to be mainly in favour of silage if the forage is to have a production as well as a maintenance function. Most of these arguments have already been advanced – the higher digestibility, net energy and protein values of material cut at an early stage of growth, the leafier and more vigorous aftermaths that follow early cutting.

One further cogent farm management point in favour of silage is that every hectare cut for silage in May and early June is a hectare less to cut for hay later in the season. A silage and hay programme spreads demands on labour and gives a comforting feeling that all eggs are not in the one conservation basket. In a bad year a farmer who does not secure the bulk of his grass crop as hay or silage by the beginning of July will have a very anxious time salvaging the wreckage that the worst sort of British summer can create.

The issue, of course, need not be one of silage versus hay. Very often in practice it is wise to make a lot of silage but some really good hay in addition. Very often our best hay-making weather comes early in the season, and if this is the case silage-making should be interrupted to make the most of the opportunity. Repeated tedding, started immediately after mowing, or the use of a flail forage harvester as a haymaking tool reduces much of the risk associated with the early cutting of hay. It pays to be an opportunist in haymaking. The longer the season of operation and the lower the target, quantitatively, the greater are the chances of making some really good hay.

However there is a growing body of dairy farmers with a convenient arrangement for feeding silage who have given up haymaking completely even to the point of buying a small quantity of hay suitable for calves in the early stages of rearing. This is a reflection of the greater confidence farmers now have in silage. Moreover it has been done without detriment to the performance and appearance of cattle and there is the added advantage of a simplified conservation programme.

SILAGE ADDITIVES

One of the features of research relating to ensilage over the past sixty years has been the quest for additives which will ensure a fermentation that is characteristic of good silage and which results in a minimum of obnoxious odours and a high level of retention of the nutrient value of the ensiled material. Victorian pioneers in silage making favoured common salt, which no doubt reflected a well-established farming belief that common salt is a panacea for many ills. It was once widely used in haymaking, particularly if material going into a rick was not completely dry. Here its function was to reduce the growth of moulds and no doubt this was the intention with ensilage.

Molasses at the rate of 6–10 kg per tonne of green material, but diluted to enable it to be applied by watering-can during the process of filling the clamp, was the most favoured additive until comparatively recently. Its function is the provision of a substrate of soluble carbohydrate to encourage a rapid lactic acid fermentation to suppress clostridial activity. It was used mainly with leguminous crops such as lucerne where undoubtedly it was efficacious in improving fermentation. However, its application is a rather messy job and therefore not a very popular one. With the present emphasis on speedy filling of silage bunkers it is little wonder that the addition of molasses is for all practical purposes a discarded technique. The only additives likely to be favoured are those, in addition to their other virtues, that can be incorporated with the herbage by means of a gravity drip applicator or by electric pump attached to the forage harvester and driven from the tractor electrics.

The main British interest in recent years has been in organic acids, in particular formic acid, not only to give greater control of the fermentation process but also to retain as high a proportion as possible of the nutritive value of the herbage at the point of ensiling. An unfortunate feature of silage, even of high quality, is that it is not only less palatable than the original herbage, thereby reducing dry-matter intake, but also there is a degree of degradation of pure protein. One result of this is that the crude protein analysis of a silage gives a poor measure of its protein-sparing function in ruminant nutrition – in other words its protein value in a total ration can be over-estimated. This is especially true if there has been any secondary clostridial fermentation which results in the breakdown of proteins to ammonia.

The incorporation of an acid or an acid aldehyde via the forage harvester results in an immediate reduction in plant respiration (which is a source of nutrient loss) and in the breakdown of proteins, while the increase in acidity reduces the likelihood of clostridial fermentation with further degradation of amino acids. These effects are reflected in animal performance and there are now many reported trials with both dairy and beef cattle that establish the superior nutritive value of treated over untreated silage.

There is no question that the use of additives, either as a straight additive or in one of its proprietary guises, has made an appreciable contribution to the biological efficiency of ensiling herbage but there are drawbacks. The acid is not particularly pleasant to handle and is also expensive, some would say unduly so. Nevertheless in the absence of anything that is more effective it is a useful standby for use when conditions are not ideal. It is our view that expensive additives are not normally essential with crops harvested in good weather during the early-summer period. Autumn-harvested crops, however, which tend to have a low sugar content are a different proposition. The addition of bacterial additives has received considerable publicity but as yet no clear-cut beneficial effect.

WILTING

Many successful farmers believe that wilting of green material to not less than 30 per cent dry matter is an essential ingredient of successful silage making. They point to the advantages which can be summarised as follows:

(a) There is more dry matter in a trailer load of a given cubic capacity and this speeds up harvesting and handling at the silo.

(b) Normally there is a better fermentation than with unwilted material, provided the silo is filled quickly and the mass consolidated to exclude air and so prevent over-heating.

(c) There is a higher intake of dry matter in wilted silage, not only because it is less bulky due to reduced moisture, but also because of greater palatability resulting from improved fermentation.

(d) There is little or no effluent. This is a very important consideration, for apart from the foul pervading smell of stale effluent there is a danger of legal action if it gets into natural watercourses.

But there are disadvantages arising from wilting:

(a) There are additional field operations as compared with

direct harvesting – cutting followed by turning and windrowing and then loading which creates difficulties, particularly in a small farm situation, but in good weather there is the compensation of an enhanced rate of removal of wilted material from the field.

(b) There is loss of dry matter in the field, particularly of over-wilted leaf.

(c) Cut grass will deteriorate more rapidly in the swathe than it will as a standing crop in bad weather. Waiting for a spell of good weather long enough for wilting to be effective can result in over-mature material.

(d) Improved animal performance from wilted as against unwilted silage has in some comparisons only been manifested where the unwilted material has been badly preserved. The chances of this happening are less with wilted material because reduction of moisture in the ensiled crop will suppress the activity of clostridial bacteria. Nevertheless there are greater respiratory losses with wilting and the true protein content of wilted silage is almost invariably low and can compare unfavourably with that of well-made silage from unwilted material.

(e) There is a greater danger of over-heating in the clamp with wilted material unless the precautions outlined below are observed, especially of heating as a result of secondary fermentation in the clamp at feeding.

Nevertheless, despite these objections, on general grounds we recommend wilting herbage before it is ensiled, except perhaps in dull catchy weather when it is highly unlikely that there will be rapid wilting. Under these conditions one should endeavour to harvest the standing crop directly and as a safeguard possibly use a formic acid type of additive to control fermentation.

SILAGE MAKING PRINCIPLES

It goes without saying that the aim is a reliable product with a high feeding value that is made as cheaply and as expeditiously as possible. This achievement is another matter but there are several well-defined principles:

(a) Silage quality is primarily limited by the quality of the ensiled herbage at the point of harvest. If the aim is a silage suitable for dairy cows, breeding ewes or fattening cattle then the crop should be cut not later than the point of ear emergence of the principal grass species. The crop will be appreciably lighter than one harvested after ear emergence (which is better suited to the needs of store cattle) but there is the compensation of quicker recovery of growth and a greater aftermath.

(b) The crop should be free of surface moisture when it goes into the silo. Wilting is only advisable when weather conditions are such that it is not a prolonged exercise with yellowing in the swathe and loss of energy value.

(c) The silo, preferably with air-tight sides, should be filled as quickly as possible and consolidated to exclude air thereby preventing any material rise in temperature. A 'wedge' system of filling the silo with overnight covering of herbage with a plastic sheet is strongly recommended to exclude oxygen and retain carbon dioxide.

(d) There is less need for an additive with material harvested in a period of sunshine which raises the sugar content of the herbage and thereby provides a better substrate for bacterial action.

(e) Experience has shown that lacerated material such as that produced by a metered chop forage harvester produces better silage than that made from longer material. This is probably due to the release of plant juices containing soluble carbohydrate and better consolidation.

(f) Once the silo is filled its contents should be consolidated and immediately covered with plastic sheeting with weighting of the sheet to ensure that it remains in position and that there are no pockets of air between it and the ensiled material. Effective weighting is essential with outside clamps in order to avoid wind damage to the sheet and entry of rain water. Old tyres are excellent weight for they are easily handled and, because they are not abrasive, they are unlikely to damage the sheeting. Silage is not cheap and it becomes even more expensive if a high proportion of the ensiled material is only fit for the muck heap. The ideal is a roofed silo but even with this the use of plastic sheeting to exclude air and prevent over-heating is an essential ingredient of good silage making.

BIG-BALE SILAGE

Like so many useful innovations in agriculture big-bale silage is the brain-wave of a practising farmer and it is creating great interest in situations where more conventional silage making is not very appropriate, e.g. on small farms where the amount of herbage that is available at any given time is not large or where the silage is destined for feeding out-wintered stock.

There are about 400–420 kg of wilted material in each bale which is enclosed in an air-tight plastic envelope. There is no deterioration of feeding value in store provided the seal is not broken. It is not generally practicable to use the plastic envelope more than once so this becomes a recurrent expense but there are compensations. For instance, there is not the expense of constructing a silo because the silage can be stored out-of-doors in close proximity to its area of use, provided it is protected from stock or the mischievous activities of small boys with sharp instruments. Vermin can be a problem if the bags are stored near an infested site for rats and mice will chew the plastic and break the seal.

Many farmers for whom big-bale silage has a particular appeal will not have the necessary baler and this part of the operation will have to be a contractor's service. Usually, though, they will have a mowing machine and a swathe turner or tedder as part of their haymaking equipment so there is not the additional expense of a forage harvester nor the need for a high powered tractor.

The aim should be a silage with a high dry matter for this, among other advantages, will reduce the number of bales to be harvested and packaged. At 20 per cent dry matter a 400 kg pack contains only 80 kg of dry matter as compared with 180 kg with a dry matter of 45 per cent. This is especially significant where a contractor is charging a fixed price for each bale. The general experience, provided the usual requisites are met, is that the silage is of good quality but once the seal has been broken, particularly with high dry-matter silage, there will be a secondary fermentation which can lead to a loss of palatability. Ideally once a pack is opened it should be consumed within the next 48 hours. Big-bale silage is an ideal method of allowing a farmer to 'start' silage making on his farm without an enormously expensive outlay on clamps and machinery. It is quickly taking over on farms in the west of the country where haymaking tends to be a hazardous operation.

TOWER SILAGE

Silage towers, especially for maize, have long been a feature of American farms and though they were an occasional installation on British farms in the 1920s there was little interest in them in the early years of the expansion in silage making that was initiated during the Second World War. It was only in the mid-sixties that steel towers, originally of American manufacture appeared on a number of farms, especially in north-east England. Ironically, American farmers visiting Britain about that time were manifesting a particular interest in the British system of storing silage in clamps, on the grounds that this not only involved a lower capital investment but was also simpler to operate and with lower maintenance costs, particularly in respect of mechanical unloading and feeding of silage.

Due to the pressure generated within the silo when it is filled rapidly, air is quickly excluded from the mass, particularly with finely chopped material, and this means that high dry matter silage can be ensiled without risks of over-heating. The usual product of these silos has a dry matter content of at least 50 per cent and this is frequently referred to as haylage.

Undoubtedly a valuable food can be produced in tower silos which is popular with the owners of some of the highest producing herds in Britain, who favour the system because of the reliability of the product. However, it is an installation for large rather than small or medium-sized herds because it is essential to spread the overheads of the very considerable investment involved in harvesting, filling, storing, unloading and distributing the product. Haylage is also a useful food for feeding cattle but again the system is only appropriate to large units.

HAYMAKING

It has long been recognised that if really good hay is to be made, conventional haymaking methods are not satisfactory, especially in the higher rainfall areas. Ironically, however, the best hay used to be made in the districts with the more difficult haymaking conditions, simply because the farmers concerned took the necessary precautions to minimise damage either by piking or using tripods. This situation has not been maintained, however, with the increasing popularity of the pick-up baler and the steady rise in labour costs.

Though nobody is likely to question the quality advantage from making hay on tripods, the time and labour involved gradually made it a very doubtful economic proposition. More and more in our farming we are being forced into a position where we have to discard an operation if it cannot be conveniently mechanised. Tripodding comes into this category, and so endeavours to safeguard the quality of the hay crop are now taking other forms, in particular 'quick' haymaking methods and the in-barn or in-stack drying of herbage baled at a stage where normally it would be considered in need of a further day's drying.

Quick haymaking may take one of two forms. The first is the more conventional one of repeated use of the tedder immediately after cutting so that the swathe is completely exposed to drying agencies. If one leaves the swathe undisturbed until it is dry on top and then turns it, especially if this is done by a finger-wheel type of machine, there will be a sad core of green material in the centre of the swathe when the rest of it is fit for baling. The finger-wheel swathe turner is an excellent machine for the purposes for which it is intended, namely turning and rowing up, but it is not a tedder.

Much of the indifferent hay made by pick-up baling is attributable to the failure of farmers to purchase an inexpensive and highly efficient power take-off driven tedder which will really fluff-up the crop. Given low humidity and sunshine with some air movement, it is reasonable to expect that a comparatively heavy crop of 4,500–5,500 kg/hectare can be made ready for baling within 72 hours from cutting, if the tedder is used to full advantage. The use of a bruiser-crimper has not become popular even though it speeded up drying time considerably by cracking and bruising stems.

The extreme in quick haymaking can be achieved by the use of the flail mower instead of the conventional mowing machine. The laceration of stems speeds up the drying process and with turning and tedding it is possible under perfect conditions to bale and cart the crop within two days of cutting. There is however an appreciable loss of the more valuable leaf. In one comparison at Cockle Park there was a loss of about 600 kg of material in a 5 tonne/hectare crop as compared with conventional mowing. However there was the compensation that the crop was harvested in good condition. In a subsequent trial, before the flailed material was harvested in good order during a short spell of fine weather but before the conventionally treated material could be baled, the weather broke and the end result was weathered hay of very poor quality.

IN-BARN DRYING

The system known in Britain as in-barn drying, and in the United States as mow-drying, has some enthusiastic supporters in this country, and with considerable justification, too, because really first-class hay can be made by this method. The process follows conventional cutting with immediate and repeated tedding until the moisture content of the material is reduced to about 40 per cent, when it can be baled, provided the sun is shining and there is a fair measure of crispness in the herbage. Under good conditions this will be some 54 hours after cutting.

The bales may be stacked, cut edge down in a chamber, if walls are available, and the air distributed through a steel mesh false floor some 50 cm above ground level. More layers of bales are added periodically to the lower layers as they dry out. Another popular alternative is to have a series of ducts branching from a main duct running the length of the Dutch barn for distributing the air. Some heat may be provided by covering the tractor or engine so that in-coming air passes over the hot engine and picks up a considerable amount of heat in this way.

If no effort is made to save quality material, there appears to be little justification for barn drying and its attendant additional expenses. However if it is regarded as a cheap half-way house to grass drying, especially on the smaller dairy farms in the high-rainfall districts or on lucerne-growing farms in the eastern counties, there is much to be said for the system. It was stressed earlier that a lot of good silage and some good hay was the best approach to pasture conservation, and there is no question but that in-barn drying is one certain method in achieving this end so far as hay is concerned.

Chapter 16

GRASSLAND SHEEP FARMING

It was suggested in Chapter 2 that one cannot generally make a strong case for sheep on a typical lowland farm that is mainly in grass. The greater biological efficiency of the dairy cow as compared with the breeding ewe along with other advantages such as better production responses to fertiliser and concentrate inputs, in an economic climate that since the late thirties has favoured milk production, puts dairying into a much higher league in terms of profitable land use. The situation is very different on hill and marginal land. The place of hardy upland sheep such as the Swaledale and the Blackface on the hills cannot be disputed and the only part that a dairy cow can play on such farms is that of being an immediate source of milk for domestic needs and providing sustenance for orphan lambs in season. Even the hardy beef breeds have a limited place on hill farms, when judged on purely biological criteria, and it is most unlikely that the present importance of breeding cattle on hill farms in Britain would have been achieved had it not been for the price and subsidy incentives for beef production that were a feature of the Government's agricultural policy during the fifties and sixties.

The situation on marginal farms, comprising land that lies between the true uplands and the more fertile lowlands, is less well defined. On the whole it is better utilised, in terms of national needs, by combinations of sheep and beef cattle than it is by dairying or cash crop production, taking into consideration the current situation in respect of surpluses of milk and cereals within EEC. However, someone on a small marginal farm cannot look at his problems in these terms – he has to make a living and dairying may be his only hope of achieving this. On the larger marginal farms there is a much better prospect for sheep as the main enterprise along with cattle which, as later discussion will underline, have an important ancillary role. Usually any cropping on such farms is mainly for forage and very often as a phase in the process of pasture improvement.

Despite the economic advantages of dairying, intensive fat lamb production can have attractions for some lowland farmers. There are those for whom the year-round pressures of dairying have reached a point where they have gladly accepted the golden handshake that Brussels has offered to dairy farmers to leave the industry. A combination of sheep and beef cattle along with some cash cropping can, in the absence of severe financial pressures, provide the sort of quiet life that is a halfway step to retirement.

Another class of lowland farm where sheep in the shape of intensive fat lamb production have a place, is one which is primarily devoted to cash cropping following a system of alternate husbandry, where a pasture phase is important as a break from cereals and an aid to the preservation of soil structure. Dairying will usually be the favoured enterprise but there can be the disability on larger farms of the herd having to walk considerable distances from pasture to milking parlour. Sheep and beef cattle on the other hand can be relatively static during the grazing season and this is a considerable advantage on awkwardly shaped farms where access to individual grazing fields sometimes presents problems. Considerations such as these may determine the choice of sheep as a grazing enterprise rather than dairy cattle, which on purely financial grounds would invariably be the more attractive option. Where a farmer has cash cropping as his main source of income sheep could nevertheless be the favoured subsidiary enterprise, not only because it is a less demanding operation but also because it involves a much lower investment in stock, specialised plant and buildings, and winter food reserves.

There is, however, one item of investment that is essential if intensive fat lamb production is to form a happy association with cash cropping and that is in sheep-proof fencing around the perimeter of grazing areas. One must be in a position to confine sheep in the field intended for them. Sheep, in particular those with a mountain ancestry in their make-up, for example the Welsh Halfbred or Mule, seem to have an infinite capacity for finding gaps and there is little joy in a sheep enterprise where one is repeatedly returning sheep to their rightful place and patching holes in a hedgerow with hurdles and old bedsteads. One of the most striking features of New Zealand sheep farms is the quality of the fencing and it pays dividends in the shape of full control of grazing, especially at those times of the year when the ewes have to be closely confined in the interests of pasture management.

ASPECTS OF PROFITABLE FAT LAMB PRODUCTION

On-farm studies of the economics of fat lamb production by the Meat and Livestock Commission stress the importance of high stocking densities and good lambing performance in determining gross margins. This is illustrated by the following table relating to lowland flocks selling lambs off grass in the summer and autumn.

Relative contributions to superiority of top third of flocks over average gross margin/hectare in 1979 (*per cent*)

Lambs reared	42
Lamb value	10
Flock replacement costs	8
Feed and forage costs	5
Stocking rate	32
Other factors	3
	100

The difference in gross margins between the average and the top one-third is substantial, £198.86 as opposed to £326.13, representing an advantage of nearly 64 per cent. The principal contributions to this superiority came from the greater number of lambs reared, primarily a reflection of superior lambing performance, and of higher stocking rate. Despite the fact that more lambs were reared per hectare, there was no erosion of the value of the individual lambs and this conflicts with the traditional belief that a sheep's worst enemy is another sheep. This belief had its foundation in the times when there were no really effective drugs to control infections, in particular parasitic infections picked up by sheep at grazing, and no meaningful knowledge concerning the biology of the important internal parasites.

Unquestionably the best quality lambs in terms of liveweight gains and finish will be achieved with ewes rearing singles on good clovery pastures at a low stocking intensity with a set grazing regime and the judicious use of store cattle that are drafted in to prevent pasture getting too rank. However, such an approach is a nonsense with present-day land values and rents. The production goal on a good lowland farm at the present time cannot be less than 20 reasonably good lambs for every hectare of grassland that is primarily devoted to the breeding flock. With the knowledge we now have of the factors involved, particularly in respect of worm control and a welcome change in emphasis away from the heavy, very prime lamb to one that is leaner and lighter, it is now feasible to market acceptable lambs off their mothers with lambing percentages in the order of 180 per cent and a stocking intensity of 10–12 ewes per hectare over the year, with a much greater intensity at the height of summer grazing.

CONTROL OF INTERNAL PARASITES

One can say categorically that the greatest single contribution that has been made since the late fifties to the intensification of fat lamb production without any detriment to the quality of lambs, has been the promotion of a clean field policy. This has been made possible by the availability of highly efficient anthelmintics and a more complete understanding of the biology of the principal internal parasites. A major advance in this area came during the period 1955–60 as a result of work by Thomas and Black at Cockle Park with *Nematodirus* spp. that had been causing a loss of thrift and mortalities in suckling lambs, especially in years with a late spring and retarded grass growth. It was a particularly serious problem on farms in the Border region which were attempting to intensify lamb production. Thomas established that Nematodirus, for all practical purposes, had an annual life cycle. Infected lambs dropped eggs on pastures during the summer and these, apparently requiring something akin to a vernalisation effect from cold winter temperatures for development, did not proceed to an infective free-living stage on pasture until the following spring. He found that if the spring is an early one with an early onset of grass growth there is a matching increase in the numbers of infective larvae on the pasture, at a stage when the lambs are young and mainly dependent on their mothers' milk and have a low grass intake. It is a very different matter in a late spring, for the peak emergence of infective larvae comes at a time when lambs are eating appreciable quantities of grass and it is in such years that clinical nematodiriasis is likely to be rife unless positive steps are taken to prevent it.

Black followed this work on the life cycle of Nematodirus in 1957–8 with a study of the effects of partial and complete resting of pastures from grazing with ewes and lambs on levels of infection and lamb performance in the following year, which fortunately from the viewpoint of the researchers, if not the lambs, was characterised by a very late spring. Treatment effects were dramatic. Where pastures were free of ewes and lambs in the previous summer there was only a negligible level of infected larvae in mid-May as compared with a massive infection on the continuously stocked treatment. Within a fortnight there was severe scouring, loss of condition and, eventually, mortalities which finally totalled 23 per cent at the 16-week stage when the average weight of survivors was only 25 kg. Where the pastures had been completely rested in the previous season there was no evidence of scouring, let alone mortalities, and an average 16-week weight of 35 kg. There were also scouring and mortalities in the partially rested treatment though not in the scale of the unrested pastures. It was very obvious that taking an early silage cut with the ensuing aftermath being grazed by lambs, even with a sub-clinical infection, was not an effective safeguard against a serious outbreak in the following season if the climatic conditions favoured a mass emergence of infected larvae when lambs were eating appreciable quantities of grass.

This work was undertaken at a time when there were no really effective drugs to combat nematodiriasis but the situation changed in the early sixties with the development of several drugs which were highly effective against a wide range of roundworms including those that have, under favourable conditions, a life cycle of no more than a few weeks. Thomas switched the emphasis in his research to the biology of the latter group. He and other workers in the same field have established a number of important facts which along with the strategic use of the effective drugs now available have given flockmasters a means of minimising losses resulting from the depredations of parasites of the gut.

In brief these are the most important facts at their disposal. Eggs derived from mature worms in the alimentary tract are passed out with the dung and they require warmth and moisture to develop. Such conditions do not occur in the winter and eggs deposited at this time perish but from spring onwards there is development to an infective free-living larvae stage which migrates from dung to grass. This development takes about 10–12 weeks in the spring but only 2–3 weeks with warmer conditions in June. The result is a high level of infection on the pastures in July–August, a time coinciding with weaning when lambs can be particularly vulnerable. If these larvae are not ingested by an unwitting host they have considerable powers of survival and can over-winter to infect lambs in the following spring and early summer. However, after the end of June of that following year the residual infection will be at a negligible level.

A further important feature is that the commonest and most important of the stomach worms invades the gut wall in the late autumn and remains there in a state of hibernation until the spring when it emerges to mature and produce eggs in what is commonly referred to as 'the spring rise'. Unless counter-measures are taken this output of eggs becomes a main source of infection of lambs later in the summer. The sensible and indeed essential course of action is to dose the ewes just after lambing as they move from their lambing accommodation to their subsequent grazing areas. This spring flush of eggs is almost eliminated with the use of modern drugs and minimal infection will develop in the suckling lambs if the ewes and lambs graze a clean field such as maiden seeds that carry no over-wintering infection.

Another time when it pays to drench ewes is in the autumn prior to tupping. Even with the best of intentions of main-taining clean grazing for the subsequent production year it may be necessary to graze ewes on some pastures in the autumn in order to prevent them from becoming too proud going into the winter or to get ewes in optimal condition for mating. Conditions will still be conducive to the development and survival of larvae until at least the beginning of November in most years and so it is advisable to drench ewes prior to their access to these pastures.

Hopefully a high proportion of lambs reared under a clean field regime will be drafted off their mothers but invariably where there are a high proportion of twins and high intensity stocking there will be a residue of lambs that require further finishing after weaning. If they are dosed at point of weaning and are then returned to their previous grazing area they will be reinfected within a few days, the degree of infection depending, of course, on the success of control measures that have been taken earlier in the production year. Ideally these weaned lambs should go either on to clean pasture or a feeding crop like forage turnips or rape for final finishing. Tail-end lambs which are likely sufferers from worm infection should not, if it is practically possible, go on to any grazing that is intended for the next season's lamb crop.

FIELD HYGIENE IN PRACTICE

A farmer following a system of alternate husbandry based on two-year leys and a sequence of tillage crops is in the fortunate position that he can have a breeding flock as his only grazing enterprise and still maintain a clean field programme. Maiden seeds, either undersown in the last cereal crop or a direct reseed following an early harvested crop such as winter barley, will logically, in its first year, provide grazing for the ewes and lambs. The second-year seeds, having provided autumn and winter keep for the ewe flock, will be used for conservation, either hay or silage, in the following summer. Freedom from sheep grazing from the end of the winter until the beginning of July will mean that the aftermath growth on the second-year seeds will, for practical purposes, be clean grazing. It will also be ideal for the store lambs with drenching following weaning at least until early September when the land will once more be required for winter corn. The ewe flock will remain on first-year seeds until such time as stubbles and the next lot of new seeds are available to take some of the grazing burden. It is reiterated that ewes should go on to these new seeds only after drenching if clean status is to be preserved for the following year.

The situation becomes rather more complicated with longer leys and permanent grass providing the grazing. Here the task of ensuring that clean swards are available for the ewe flock becomes considerably easier if cattle are introduced into the system. A combination of maiden seeds and older pastures grazed by cattle and used for conservation in the previous year will provide the necessary clean grazing. In the following year this area in its turn would be grazed by cattle or used for conservation. The balance between cattle and sheep would obviously vary with the farm and the type of the cattle enterprise but, in general terms sheep if they are properly managed, are likely to be the more profitable members of the partnership unless a farmer is a very skilled buyer of store cattle.

IMPORTANCE OF PROLIFIC EWES

Britain is fortunate in having several very prolific breeds of sheep and, in appropriate crosses, this prolificacy seems to be enhanced. For instance it is not uncommon for an age-balanced flock of Mules (Bluefaced Leicester × Swaledale or Scotch Blackface) to average two lambs born and the Scottish and Welsh Halfbred are not far behind in respect of their fecundity. Moreover, in common with other crossbreeds with a parent hill breed they are exceptionally good mothers. It is not unreasonable with good management to expect an average of 180 per cent based on ewes put to the tup and lambs reared, a performance which makes visiting Antipodean farmers green with envy. The average New Zealand fat lamb producer, working with Romneys or Corriedales is very well pleased with 120 per cent, though it must be conceded that these sheep have fleeces at least 2 kg heavier than those of their British counterparts. However, meat is relatively much more valuable than wool under British conditions and so it is economic sense to put the emphasis on weight of lambs produced per ewe, a function of numbers reared and weight for age in the lambs.

High prolificacy has another important advantage under British conditions, namely that ewes rearing twins are at least 60 per cent more efficient users of food than those rearing singles. Moreover this economy has a particular significance in the winter months when the grazing is minimal and expensive supplementary feeding is necessary, particularly in the later stages of pregnancy. In practice, because there is no cheap and reliable method of diagnosing multiple pregnancies, all ewes are fed the same until they have lambed. It is only then that one is able to give preferential treatment to ewes rearing twins, but by then spring is on the way and with it the prospect of ample grass. When this point is reached the high-fecundity flock comes into its own for then there are the maximum number of mouths capable of making good use of the rapid upsurge of growth.

Seldom in farming does one get something for nothing and so it is where there is a high proportion of twins, for they are much more vulnerable than singles to internal parasitic infections. This is understandable because a single lamb has a higher intake of the ewe's milk as compared with twins. Not only is there the direct nutritional benefit of this additional milk but adult sheep, with an age tolerance of worm infections, in a sense act as disinfecting agents just as cattle do when they graze with sheep. Where the ratio of adults to juveniles is a wide one, as it is where most of the ewes are rearing twins, then it is of paramount importance that the flock has clean grazing. If the circumstances are such that it is not possible to provide this for the whole flock it is sensible to separate ewes with singles from those with doubles and put the latter on young grass or any other available pasture that has not been grazed by infected sheep in the previous year.

Though the level of prolificacy of a flock is, in the ultimate, determined by genetic factors it is also profoundly affected by environmental factors and of these the nutritional status of the ewe is of paramount importance. This has been clearly established through flock studies by the Meat and Livestock Commission whose field staff have made an assessment of the body condition of ewes at mating, scoring them on a scale established by Australian research workers, and then has related these scores to subsequent lambing performance. A consistent picture emerges for a wide range of breeds and crosses, namely that the fitter the ewes are at mating the greater will be the proportion of multiple births provided the ewes are not grossly over-fat. Here not only is there some tailing off in prolificacy but also there is a needless waste of food while very fat ewes seem to be more vulnerable in late pregnancy to inversion of the vagina and pregnancy toxaemia. They also have the unfortunate habit of becoming 'cast', that is lying on their backs unable to get back on their feet unless they are given assistance.

The picture emerging from the MLC studies has materially altered prescriptions for the management of ewes between weaning and mating. At one time it was considered sufficient to 'flush' ewes by putting them on good grazing about two to three weeks prior to joining the rams. Prior to this they were often required in the 10–12 weeks following weaning to clear rough pastures or to subsist on very short commons such as stubbles or even moorland grazing. Now it is realised that this is too harsh a nutritional regime, particularly for ewes that are low in condition as a result of rearing twins. Once the ewes are completely dry, generally about a fortnight after weaning, they should be sorted on the basis of their condition, and the poorer ewes, which will generally have mothered twins, should immediately go on to good grazing to ensure that they are in prime condition at mating some ten weeks later. Any ewes that are in prime condition at sorting, which will usually be the mothers of singles that have been drafted before the main body of the lambs, can be asked to work a little harder for their living without detriment to their conception rate, provided they come on to good grazing at least three weeks before they go to the ram.

Good grazing conditions should be maintained for at least a month following mating for a severe check at this time can result in embryonic mortalities. It is a different story during the middle part of pregnancy, from the 6th to the 14th week. This is a time when the flock can be 'mob-stocked', that is concentrated in a rotational pattern of grazing in order to eat out pastures so that there will be a clean start for subsequent spring growth. Good nutrition during the last six weeks of pregnancy is critical in the avoidance of pregnancy toxaemia and ensuring that there are not only strong lambs at birth but also an adequate supply of milk to give them a good start in life. By this stage, with heavy stocking and the need to have clean pastures for the ewes after lambing, it is most unlikely, under British conditions, that grazing will make a significant contribution to flock maintenance after the turn of the year until the start of spring. However, grass in the shape either of hay or silage can continue to be the major nutritional component. It is stressed that these must be high-quality products in order to maximise nutrient intake but even with these some supplementary concentrate feeding is essential with the prospect of a high proportion of multiple birth if neo-natal mortalities are to be minimised.

IN-WINTERING OF EWES

In theory a hectare of well-managed pasture, under good lowland conditions, will produce sufficient nutrients, along with some supplementary concentrates, to maintain at least twelve breeding ewes plus their lambs up to their normal point of disposal. In practice, because of a variety of reasons such stocking rates are rarely achieved. One of these reasons is winter poaching of pastures which impairs subsequent growth in April and May when there is the greatest grazing pressure on a heavily stocked farm.

We investigated the effects of winter treading on subsequent growth in a trial at Cockle Park in the early sixties when we were making a study of the feasibility of in-wintering. A 10 ewe/hectare intensity for the early part of the winter and a 20 ewe/hectare intensity for the latter part of the winter (to simulate farm conditions where one rests half of the grassland from the turn of the year to give a fresh bite for the ewes after lambing) reduced grass production by one-fifth up to the end of May, as compared with the paddocks that were completely bared in the autumn but rested from the New Year. This occurred in an exceptionally dry winter on a dense ryegrass sward in its fifth year. If it had been a more typical winter with snow followed by thaws as well as occasional heavy rain the land would have been poached black and the sward would have suffered irreparable damage.

It is our belief, and this view is shared by an increasing body of farmers that with intensive fat lamb production on strong land in-wintering must be an integral part of the system. It need not involve expensive buildings, on the contrary, for breeding ewes cannot carry high capitalisation costs. A partly-covered concrete yard with a covered area for straw bedding or a modification of existing buildings can be adequate provided they are well ventilated to eliminate the risk of pneumonia. It is also advisable to subdivide the flock in lots of not more than 25–30 ewes according to condition and expected time of lambing and to provide adequate trough and rack space to prevent injury to unborn lambs at feeding times. Electric lighting makes night-time surveillance over lambing that much easier and individual lambing pens to accommodate ewes and their lambs until they are safely established together are essential.

In-wintering has many advantages apart from protection of pastures and not the least is the comfort of the shepherd and sheep in bad weather especially at lambing. With sound management of the unit there is a minimal loss of lambs following birth and this is of considerable economic import-ance now that spare lambs sold for fostering can at two to three days old realise twice the price of a fat lamb prior to Britain's entry into EEC. On a tillage farm sacrifice fields for over-wintering are no longer necessary and these can go into the more profitable autumn-sown corn rather than spring-sown crops. As they have protection from climatic or nutritional stress it is reasonable to keep old ewes that would normally be culled for an extra year provided they have sound udders. Ewe depreciation is usually the greatest single cost in fat lamb production and this is one means of reducing it.

It is advisable to keep ewes and newly-born lambs in a protected area for several days following lambing before turning them out to pasture. This is a very necessary precaution where rubber rings are applied to young lambs for tailing and castration, because male lambs in particular can be mismothered in a large field and without milk in their bellies they are very vulnerable to weather hazards.

SYSTEMS OF GRAZING

A number of years ago a farm-scale comparison was made over several seasons at Ruakura Research Station in New Zealand to determine ewe and lamb performance under two contrasted regimes of set-stocking and rotational grazing. Reference has been made to the results in Chapter 7 under the section headed Fat Lamb Production (page 98). At the end of the trial the findings were summarised as follows: If a sheep farmer is comfortably placed financially in that there is no great pressure for him to maximise output then he could be well satisfied with a simple non-rotational system with only moderate stocking intensity. On the other hand, if it is important to raise returns per unit then the greater control possible with closer subdivision and appropriate movement of stock permits a farmer to lift stocking intensities with only an acceptable diminution of individual animal performance.

The situation of the typical British flockmaster is very much that of the latter category of the New Zealand sheep farmer. If a sheep enterprise is to be a paying proposition, able to stand comparison with alternative enterprises, then it is essential to maximise production within the limits set by the law of diminishing returns. This does not necessarily mean that the British farmer should follow a system of rotational grazing, for his circumstances differ from those of a typical New Zealand fat lamb producer who has to maintain a low cost system based almost entirely on permanent grass that will never receive the stimulus of artificial nitrogen and ewes that will never have the pleasure of eating trough food. These two tools give a flexibility in nutritional planning that materially affects choice of grazing options.

The position also differs according to the type of farm. For instance, close subdivision to permit some form of controlled grazing may be suitable for a livestock farm that is principally in old grass but it would be inappropriate on a mainly cropping farm with a short-duration grass break. Here the most one can expect is secure perimeter fencing of field units that are of a convenient size for tillage and possibly some limited division of the grass block with temporary fencing. Equation of stock appetite and grass growth may be more economically achieved by the judicious use of nitrogen and concentrate supplementation rather than by a heavy investment in temporary subdivisions and water availability that is necessary for intensive rotational grazing.

Cattle can also be used as temporary adjuncts to control grazing so that it is of the right quality for sheep which thrive better with a dense leafy sward rather than rank pasture that is running to stem. There is an old saying of sheep-men on Romney Marsh that if anyone drops a sixpence on one of its famed fattening pastures he should be able to retrace his footsteps to find it. Another saying relating to the two-year-old wethers that once grazed these pastures was that they should eat by day the grass that had grown the night before. These, of course, were exaggerations for the sake of emphasis but there is no doubt that a dense leafy sward such as that provided by

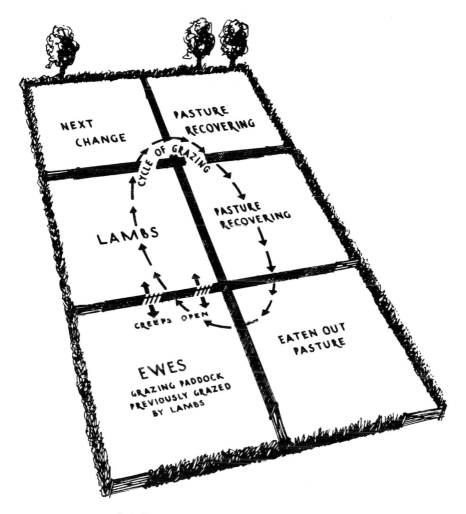

FIG. 2

Arrangements of paddocks for forward-creep grazing.

a well-managed combination of a small-leaved white clover, such as Kent wild white or S184, and a prostrate pasture-type ryegrass such as Melle (which has the added virtue of being reasonably palatable) provides ideal grazing for ewes and lambs.

The issue whether to adopt set-stocking or rotational grazing is in our view of lesser significance than the importance of planning a grass utilisation programme so that there is always an annual successsion of clean grazing for ewes and lambs. Generally the grazing system that favours this objective is the one that should be adopted.

CREEP GRAZING

The last edition of this book had a chapter on creep grazing which at one time was thought to be an effective method of lamb production at apprecially higher stocking intensities than would be considered practicable either with set-stocking or rotational grazing. The concept was based on an observation that a ewe's milk flow peaks at 2–3 weeks but falls to about half this level at 8–9 weeks. Meanwhile the lambs' appetite is increasing as the mothers' efficiency as converters of grass into milk for their lambs is declining. This is unimportant at stocking intensities of 10–12 ewes per hectare when there is ample grass for both ewes and lambs, but it is a different matter with 20–22 ewes plus lambs per hectare for then ewes are taking good grass which would be better used directly by the lambs in the last 6–8 weeks before weaning.

Forward creep grazing was devised at Cockle Park in 1955–6 to get the best use of grass. The flock was grazed on a six-paddock rotation so arranged that from the point when lambs started to graze they had prior access through creep gates to the next paddock in the rotation (see Figure 2). During the first 7–8 weeks the flock was rotated according to the needs of the ewes but progressively after that their role became that of scavengers behind their lambs at a time when pasture was tending to run to stem. Once the system was established at Cockle Park it was subsequently tested commercially at the University of Newcastle's Nafferton Farm, where over a long succession of years using flocks of 200–250 ewes outputs in excess of 900 kg of liveweight per hectare were consistently obtained from Suffolk × Scottish Halfbred lambs over the period April to mid-July inclusive. The stocking rate was usually of the order of 20–22 ewes and 34–36 lambs per hectare with up to half the lambs being drafted fat off their mothers.

The system created interest in the early sixties when there were a number of practitioners who had variable success according to the degree of attention paid to essential management details, but twenty years later forward creep grazing has to all intents and purposes become a ship that passed in the night. There are several reasons for its decline. Firstly it was developed at a time when there was a declining interest in fat lamb production. It was also a time when the fat stock certification scheme, which determined whether lambs would be eligible for deficiency payments under the guaranteed price scheme, favoured heavy prime lambs that would have been down-graded under the conditions operating twenty years later. Creep grazing did not produce this class of lamb but a leaner, lighter type which by the standards at that time required further finishing. Most important of all the attention to essential details necessary for success seemed to be beyond the average fat lamb producer who preferred a less complicated system. Then there was also the expense and inconvenience of re-erecting temporary fencing on clean grazing every year. Whether it will ever achieve any place in the British sheep industry because of further pressure to intensify fat lamb production is a very moot point. As matters stand, creep grazing seems to be a good idea on paper but not in practice.

GENERAL MANAGEMENT CONSIDERATIONS

Several management factors have been stressed including the choice of naturally prolific ewes, handled in such a way as to give full expression to this trait, the importance of grazing free of worm infections and ensuring that grass output, particularly in the early spring, is not impaired by winter poaching. This has led in turn to a stressing of the value of in-wintering of ewes not only for the protection of swards on heavy lands but also for its ancillary benefits. In essence our aim has been to establish a pattern of management that ensures a high output of lambs in respect of both numbers and quality. These, as MLC studies have shown, have a major influence on gross margins achieved per ewe.

The average price realised for lambs is also affected by time of lambing. MLC farm studies in 1979 revealed on average a 16 per cent advantage in price realised per lamb in early as opposed to later lambing flocks with summer and autumn sales of grass. There is of course an added cost in early lambing in the shape of higher supplementation especially of concentrates and this must be taken into account. Nevertheless it can be more profitable on early farms to lamb in February and early March in order to take advantage of the appreciably higher prices realised up to about mid-July which usually heralds a sharp decline in sale values.

However, our advice to farmers on late land, especially at high intensities of stocking, is to lamb about 2–3 weeks before the expected onset of spring growth for with this timing one usually gets the best coincidence between flock appetite and the availability of pasture.

Worms, it is stressed, are not the only potential problem facing the intensive fat lamb producer. There is that ubiquitous group of clostridial bacteria which live in the soil and which in various forms are responsible for a number of killer diseases such as lamb dysentery, pulpy kidney, braxy, tetanus, struck and blackleg. Fortunately there are now effective vaccines available to help combat these diseases including a multiple vaccine that can be administered to the pregnant ewe to give protection via colostrum to lambs up to 10–12 weeks.

Footrot is not a killer disease but it can be responsible for a considerable loss of thrift. It is, however, a disease that can be eliminated because the organism responsible does not survive on pasture for more than 2–3 weeks. A programme of treatment and isolation of affected animals, routine trimming of hooves, the use of 5–10 per cent formalin in footbaths and returning only clean sheep to clean pastures can put paid to the disease as many sheepfarmers have now proved to their absolute satisfaction. Intensive sheep farming on pasture has indeed come a very long way since those days when there was some validity in the view that a sheep's worst enemy at pasture was another sheep.

Chapter 17

BEEF FROM GRASS

Traditionally there were two main types of beef production in Britain, yard feeding mostly on arable products that provided the bulk of winter and spring beef (and in the process produced muck then considered to be an essential ingredient in successful crop production) and grass finishing of store cattle during the summer and autumn. Throughout Britain there were permanent pastures, dominantly ryegrass and white clover associations, that were renowned for their feeding qualities and possibly the best-known of these were to be found in the strong land of the Midlands notably in the Welland valley where a very careful management procedure, developed through experience over many generations was scrupulously followed. The best of these pastures would be stocked at the rate of about a bullock to the acre in the spring and as they were drafted fat they would be replaced by further stores which possibly had been grazing other pastures on the same farm that were not of prime feeding quality. The best of these fattening pastures were capable of producing about 500 kg of liveweight increase per hectare over a seven-month grazing season. Choice of store animals and stocking rates were very important. The desired situation was one where bullocks could fill their bellies fairly quickly and then lie down to ruminate. Set-stocking was always practised and it was important that cattle suffered the minimum of disturbance. Rising 3-year-old and even older bullocks were preferred on the grounds that these pastures were too strong for younger animals. Ireland was a principal source of favoured stores and these had another advantage in that they were, for the most part, out-wintered and therefore acclimatised to grazing conditions. This was important because they put on flesh immediately whereas soft, in-wintered animals lost their initial bloom in the course of adjusting to a different environment. Cattle were removed from these pastures in the late autumn to avoid damage from poaching, which could be very harmful on strong land with a high water table. Sheep were often used for a final trimming of the fattening fields before they were then left undisturbed until the following spring.

The expertise required for financial success on these feeding farms embraced much more than the adjustment of stocking rates to maximise liveweight gains. Graziers had also to be skilled buyers and sellers of stock at a time when the average farmer was operating on a feeder's margin of little more than a five pound note. It was the man who could buy stores to best advantage to sell them at a premium 4–5 months later who was able to keep in business in those precarious years before the advent of guaranteed prices. From the outside, grass feeding may have seemed to be a simple uncomplicated operation following a well-defined pattern which was sometimes referred to rather disparagingly as 'dog and stick farming' but in fact it was, and still is for those that remain in the business, a highly skilled operation.

Grass feeding, in common with other branches of beef production, went into a decline when food was rationed and the emphasis in domestic agriculture was on food crops either for direct human consumption or for feeding dairy cattle, for milk was rightly adjudged to be a first priority in animal production. As part of the war-time drive for more cereals ploughing-up orders were placed on many of the recognised feeding pastures and this created consternation among the affected farmers, because of a belief that the intrinsic capacity of these pastures to put flesh on stock would be lost irreparably.

There was so much concern about this that the Royal Agricultural Society commissioned a study to compare the value of leys and permanent pastures for beef production. The results were predictable. The ploughing-out policy was fully justified where the comparison was between low-quality permanent grass and leys based on reliable seeds which were adequately fertilised. However, at the other end of the scale, at similar stocking rates, there appeared to be little between the two types of pasture except that the permanent swards retained greater leafiness through the summer. This is a well-defined attribute of permanent pastures that have been retained under a grazing regime over a number of years and as a consequence consist of leafy ecotypes. On the other hand leys, especially those based on ryegrass, tend to have a stemmy phase in mid-summer unless they are hard grazed, which is not consistent with maximising rate of gain in feeding cattle.

CHANGES IN BEEF PRODUCTION

A debate on the relative merits of young and old grass is largely academic now that the specific roles of the two categories of grass are more widely understood. Pressure to plough up old grass, since entry into EEC, has come not from Government directives but from the very favourable returns from cereal and rape seed production. There are still some grass fatteners who are very much in the mould of the old Midland graziers but now the emphasis is on much younger and more intensively grazed cattle. The demand for heavy, well-finished animals has fallen progressively with the increasing preference for lean, tender beef, apart from that going into the hamburger trade which must also be lean but in addition have some age on it. This trade and also that for manufacturing meats provides the main outlet for animals that have served their time in dairy or beef breeding herds.

Ironically, the modern approach to beef production from grass owes a great deal to the one-time popular innovation of the late fifties known as barley beef which was the brain-child of T. R. Preston, then at the Rowett Research Institute. In brief, Preston converted Friesian calves which had been reared to 12 weeks on the early-weaning system (which he largely devised) into very acceptable slaughter animals at twelve months of age with a liveweight of approximately 400–420 kg and a carcass yield of over 60 per cent on an *ad lib* diet of rolled barley fortified with proteins, minerals and vitamins. Their efficiency of food use was remarkably good and Preston calculated that a typical crop of barley giving 4·5 tonnes/hectare could be converted into 900–1,000 kg of liveweight gain under his barley beef system. This he emphasised to the discomforture of grassland enthusiasts was about double the normal expectation of liveweight gain from grass feeding.

There was an immediate response from the grassland side and workers at the Grassland Research Institute at Hurley mounted a project which aimed at producing twelve-month beef off grass. They used autumn-born Hereford × Friesian steers which were yard-fed in their first winter and then run on intensively managed pasture with surplus grass being conserved as silage. Some animals were drafted for slaughter at 400–430 kg in the autumn but the seasonal decline in grass growth and quality had set in before the majority of the animals were ready for grading. Silage was fed to them and though liveweight increases per hectare comparable with those postulated by Preston were eventually achieved it became obvious that grass alone was not the answer, even with Hereford × Friesian steers which are much earlier mating than pure Friesians.

Simultaneously studies were being undertaken at other centres on what eventually became a sensible compromise between barley beef and the complete reliance on pasture that Hurley workers had originally envisaged. These led to what is now generally known as the 18-month system which owes a great deal in its evolution and extension to the pioneering efforts of a Northumbrian farmer, Fenwick Jackson. It grew in popularity as barley beef declined, largely as a result of its great initial success. As more and more people got on the barley beef band-wagon good Friesian calves which had been freely available at £8–£10 apiece soon doubled and trebled in price in response to the enhanced demand and barley became appreciably dearer. Additionally it became evident that there was not an unlimited demand for barley beef, which for many palates was too bland a product as compared with beef from somewhat older animals killed at live weights of 500 kg or more. They also gave a better spread of the overheads arising from the initial cost of calves than barley beef at 400 kg liveweight.

However, barley beef contributed much more than a stimulus to the production of beef from grass. It helped materially in establishing the suitability of Friesian calves for beef production and it demonstrated how economies can be made in food use by reaching the desired condition and weight at an early age. For instance a 250 kg carcass at 12 months of age represents a much more economical use of food than a 350 kg carcass at 24 months with an extra 12 months of maintenance added to feeding costs. An extension of the feeding period can only be justified economically when a cheaper food is substituted for a more expensive one and this is what happens with the 18-month system which is largely based on grass.

Perhaps the largest contribution made by barley beef to beef production generally was an indirect one, in that it introduced a greater measure of economic discipline into the industry. There was, for the first time, the possibility of following growth performance under reasonably controlled conditions and of measuring food intakes. In these respects barley beef production was more akin to pig production than it was to the more traditional forms of beef production, which nevertheless benefited from a greater awareness of the importance of measuring inputs and their responses. This was stimulated by the establishment in the mid-sixties of the Beef Recording Association (which was later incorporated in the Meat and Livestock Commission) and for the first time commercial beef producers were given appropriate production standards and targets.

Out of this came a greater awareness of the importance of weight for age, not only in comparisons between breeds and crosses, but also within breeds and this was reflected in the support given by progressive beef breeders to official performance testing. Progressively, commercial beef men moved away from the early maturing breeds like the Aberdeen Angus, first to the Hereford and later to the introduced Continental breeds in particular the Charolais. It was in this period of change that the 18-month systems of beef production were developed.

AUTUMN-BORN DAIRY BEEF

The autumn-born calf is a somewhat different proposition from those born in the spring which will be discussed in the next section. Regardless of time of birth most dairy-bred calves are now reared on an early-weaning system where they receive milk (or more commonly a milk substitute) for up to 4–5 weeks after which they go completely on to solid food. This includes, as well as concentrates, an increasing proportion of silage or hay, which, incidentally, must be of very good quality to maintain the target of an increase of 0·65–0·7 kg per day and a liveweight of 200 kg at 6–7 months of age when they go out to grass.

The change to grass feeding should be gradual. Unlike single-suckled calves at grass they have, at turning out, no grazing experience and they will spend most of their first day outside careering around the field with their tails in the air. Trough feeding should be continued until the calves have settled to grazing but normally it can be terminated after 2–3 weeks, though some farmers continue with a grain supplement throughout the summer. Experimental studies on this point have established no appreciable advantage from this sup plementation of autumn-born calves under good grazing conditions because the small advantage at subsequent yarding soon disappears, apparently as a result of compensatory growth by the unsupplemented animals.

Precautions must be taken against worm infections right

from the outset and the starting point is the administration of an oral vaccine against husk before the calves go out to grass followed by a suitable anthelmintic in July to control stomach and intestinal worms. It if is practically possible the calves should graze pastures that did not carry calves in the previous summer and for this reason this style of beef production fits in well with a fat lamb enterprise which has a similar requirement for clean grazing.

It is possible with good pastures and a nitrogen regime of about 250 units/hectare to carry up to three beasts per hectare and save enough silage for their winter needs from this area. Normally at least two-thirds of the allocated pasture can go for first-cut silage, with the second-cut silage also acting as a cleaning operation, coming from the first grazed area and part of the ungrazed area. The aim must be a high-class product, cut at an early stage and wilted to maximise dry-matter intake and thereby economise on concentrate use. The whole area will be available for grazing after mid-July and it should suffice until well into the autumn. It is preferable to yard cattle before mid-October because if they remain outside for too long they grow hide and hair and lose flesh. It is advisable to feed about 1½–2 kg of rolled barley daily during their last few weeks outside to compensate for the declining quality and palatability of autumn grass. A slightly higher rate of supplementation will usually be necessary at yarding of 2–4 kg of barley according to the quality of the silage, and though grass silage apparently has ample protein it is advantageous to include 5–10 per cent of soya meal in the rolled barley mix because of the degradation of the grass protein as a result of ensiling. Usually cattle make only limited gains during their first month inside, but from December onwards daily liveweight increases of at least 1 kg are attained on silage *ad lib*, plus 2–3 kg of barley mixture daily.

Pure Friesian steers will usually be at least 18 months before they have the required weight and finish and this also applies

to Charolais and Simmental Friesian crosses. Hereford ×
Friesian steers are earlier maturing at rather lower weights
and it is convenient to have a proportion of these in the annual
throughput, in order to reduce the size of the feeding lots and
give the additional trough space that steers will require
towards the end of their feeding period.

In summary the following are reasonable targets with the 18-
month system based on autumn-born, Friesian-type calves.

Month	Stage	Weight (kg)	Diet	Daily gain (kg)
Oct–Nov	Birth–5 weeks	40–60	Colostrum then milk substitute, hay and early weaning mix to appetite	0·6
Nov–Dec	5–12 weeks	60–110	Hay and early weaning mix to appetite	0·65
Jan–April	12–28 weeks	110–200	Hay and/or silage to appetite, 2 kg concentrates	0·8
April–Oct	28–52 weeks	200–340	Grazing with 2 kg barley for first 2 and last 3 weeks	0·85
Oct–April	52–78 weeks	340–520	Good silage to appetite 2–3 kg cereal mix daily	0·85

The above targets are exceeded by many producers, for
instance Fenwick Jackson regularly averaged 0·85 kg liveweight gain over the whole rearing and finishing period, and
this achievement is matched by his brother Edward, farming
near Alnwick who in 1981 won the MLC–British Grassland
Society Grass-to-Meat Award for the Northern Section.
Phillip Jones of West Haddon, Northampton, in winning the
Eastern Section Award, averaged 0·9 kg daily liveweight gain
at grass with a stocking rate of 4·2 head/hectare. Both farmers

achieved a liveweight production in excess of 1,200 kg/hectare and a gross margin of over £600/hectare at a time when a £400/hectare gross margin was generally considered to be satisfactory for dairy-bred cattle.

Since the late seventies two factors have reduced the attractiveness of 18-month beef. The first has been the steady increase in the proportion of North American Holstein blood in British dairy herds and these rather angular animals, despite high growth rates, do not compare on conformation with the straight British Friesian and this is reflected in their selling price. The sad fact is that good black and white calves are now becoming very difficult to acquire. The second factor is the nature of the cash flow and the very high capitalisation associated with the intensive 18-month system which has been exacerbated by the high level of interest rates for bank overdrafts. Where the farmer covers the whole operation from early rearing to finishing he has to finance two lots of cattle for up to six months of the year. At peak just after the turn of the year the capitalisation with a stocking rate of three per hectare during the summer could, at 1983 values, amount to as much as £1,600/hectare. The investment pressure can be reduced by purchasing calves at 3–4 months of age but this means that someone else is taking the profit for this phase of production. Again the financial burden can be lightened by selling a proportion at the yearling stage in order to keep the bank manager contented and fortunately there is a good demand for forward stores off grass.

There is much to be said for not having all one's eggs in the one pasture-utilisation basket by combining 18-month beef and intensive fat lamb production. Apart from the value of having two kinds of grazing animal in maintaining a clean pasture programme, sheep have a lower capitalisation per unit area and there is a better cash flow through having the two enterprises. In addition an age-balanced flock is a useful hedge against inflation.

DAIRY BEEF – WINTER- AND SPRING-BORN CALVES

The thriftiest calves at pasture on the 18-month system are normally those weighing at least 200 kg at turn-out for they are sufficiently well-developed to make good use of grazing. It is not possible with December and later-born calves to attain this weight at the start of the grazing season and this necessitates a different type of management. It is advisable to delay turning out till May and even June in the case of March-born calves. A silage aftermath in a well-sheltered field is ideal for the purpose. Calves as young as this are very selective grazers and it is most unlikely that they will effectively control the pasture, which must provide clean leafy grazing for reasonable thrift. The aftermath of a second-cut silage field help preserve the continuity of fresh clean pasture. It is advisable to give a cereal supplement while these calves are at pasture and 1·5 kg of straight rolled barley without any protein additive will be adequate, except when drought limits the availability of grazing and necessitates a higher rate of supplementation. A reasonable expectation for February-born Friesian or cross-Friesian calf, turned out to grass towards the end of May, is a liveweight gain of 0·7 kg/day over a grazing period terminating at the beginning of October, when yarding is the best prescription for this class of beast which by then should weigh at least 200 kg.

The barley supplement can be continued along with silage to appetite for the first month after yarding when they will have settled to their new environment. If the silage is of the quality prescribed for finishing cattle in the preceding section, it is debatable whether it is economic to continue the barley feeding. There is no prospect of finishing them in the yards and it should be possible to average slightly better than 0·5 kg/day of liveweight increase on silage alone to give a big framed store of about 300 kg liveweight at point of turnout in April. This is the sort of store that will make compensatory growth of the order of a kg/day over a 6-month grazing season. It is unlikely that pure Friesians or Charolais × Friesians will be in slaughter condition by the autumn unless they have a cereal supplement from about the beginning of August because they have a tendency to keep growing with back-end grass as their sole feed. The probability is that unsupplemented cattle will require yarding in October to finish in December–January at about 22 months of age. Hereford × Friesians are a different proposition because of their fattening propensity and they will finish at grass from August onwards at somewhat lower weights, 420–450 kg as compared with the Friesians at 510–550 kg some four months later. The probability is that Friesians will leave the greater profit because of their greater weight and the appreciably higher initial cost of the Hereford-cross calves, unless the Frieisans have an obvious infusion of Holstein blood to the detriment of their sale value.

FINISHING OF SINGLE-SUCKLED WEANERS

There was a time when the great majority of single-suckled calves were spring-born but for a variety of reasons, which will be discussed in the following section, a substantial proportion of herds now consist predominantly of autumn- and early-winter calvers. Usually calves on these farms will have been weaned for as long as 8–10 weeks prior to the October calf sales which are a popular outlet for this class of stock and at this stage they will usually be first class material for winter finishing. Not only will they have the necessary size and frame but also they will have recovered from the inevitable post-weaning check and they will start to thrive immediately after yarding. Most breeders will feed some trough food following weaning and this is another plus because it is a step towards familiarising them for winter feeding, especially where this is based on silage and cereal supplement. This is now generally a favoured form of winter feeding except where a main reliance is still placed on roots and arable by-products, which continue to be important on mainly arable farms, that put a high value on FYM for potato or sugar beet production.

Where silage is the basis, food management differs very little from that during the last winter with dairy beef. Again there is the need for high-quality silage preferably with easy feeding rather than self-feeding in order to maximise intake. Increasingly feeders are using forage wagons to deliver a silage-cereal mix into troughs and this among other advantages ensures that individual cattle get a fair share of their concentrate allowance. It is important to have cattle in matched lots for size and steers should be separated from heifers. The latter are the earlier maturing and normally they will be marketable from mid-December onwards until February, when usually a start can be made on drafting the steers. It is false economy to hold cattle once they are in slaughter condition in the hope of getting heavier carcasses. Much of this additional weight will be fat which neither butcher nor housewife wants and it is also expensively produced in terms of efficiency of food use.

Slaughter weights will vary according to breed and sex. Heifers are appreciably lighter than steers at any given age and they will usually go for slaughter at anything up to 100 kg less than steers on a similar feeding regime. Unquestionably Charolais-cross weaners are now the preferred material for yard finishing because of their better growth and their capacity to reach heavy weights without becoming unacceptably fat. A 12-month Charolais steer out of a typical Irish cow at point of yarding will usually weigh at least 380 kg which gives an advantage of 30–40 kg over a comparable Hereford and rather more than this over an Aberdeen Angus.

Hereford-cross steers should put on at least 0.9 kg/day on a diet of good silage and 1·5–2·5 kg of concentrates daily and reach a slaughter weight of 430–450 kg at 16–17 months of age. Charolais-cross steers are capable of making somewhat higher daily gains. Under good conditions they are capable of averaging as high as 1·2 kg/day, but 1 kg/day is a more typical figure leading to slaughter weights of 500–580 kg at 16–18 months of age.

Of the later-born suckled calves any heifer of at least 255 kg, or steer that is about 50 kg heavier at weaning, can be regarded as suitable candidates for yard-finishing at 15–17 months but lighter animals, which will largely have been dropped well after the New Year, will be more profitably wintered on what is essentially a store diet, gaining possibly not more than 0·6 kg/day before being turned out to grass as reasonably strong stores. Hereford and Limousin-cross steers which go to grass at 15 months should be at least 350 kg and Charolais or Simmental crosses should be 30–50 kg heavier. Silage by itself is fully capable of maintaining the desired rate of growth during the winter if it is of reasonable quality but it is advisable to check-weigh representative animals at intervals and to enrich their ration by feeding some concentrates if target gains have not been achieved. It is stressed that there is no advantage in having a lot of bloom on cattle when they go out to grass for this will soon be lost when they experience the impact of our typical April weather. They are all the better for a little weather on their backs during the winter and partly open yards have something to offer on this account with this class of cattle.

Once they have settled to pasture their management will essentially be the same as that for spring-born dairy stores over their last summer. They will finish more quickly with set-stocking and the minimum of disturbance on a leafy ryegrass-clover association which is better for feeding than a grass-dominant sward that develops with heavy nitrogen usage, for the latter is a growing rather than a fattening sward. Hereford or Aberdeen-cross heifers will be the first to finish and some will be fit by the end of June. Steers will follow about 6–8 weeks after heifers but in both instances Charolais and Simmental crosses, especially the steers, will not be ready until the autumn when it may be advisable to give them a cereal supplement say 1·5–2 kg of rolled barley per day to finish them at grass. Under some circumstances it may be necessary to yard the tail-end steers and finish them for the premium Christmas market at about 600 kg liveweight.

BULL BEEF AND HORMONES

Beef from males that have been deliberately left entire to secure more rapid growth and leaner carcasses, as compared with castrates, does not have the popularity in Britain it has long enjoyed in many Continental countries and more recently in Australia and New Zealand where it helps to increase the supply of suitable beef for the apparently insatiable American appetite for hamburgers. There are several reasons for this and one has been the deliberate discouragement of the practice by the Government with a calculated campaign of bureaucratic restraint.

Another factor is the way beef cattle are handled in Britain. Whereas the Continentals mainly stall feed bulls which are firmly tied by the neck this seldom applies in Britain because of our preference either for yard feeding in the winter or for free grazing in the summer. There is a danger, particularly with bulls of dairy breeds, of their becoming fractious from about the yearling stage onwards. This does not matter with barley beef where yarded animals seldom exceed twelve months at slaughter and it is in this system where bull beef is of potential value but it is a different story with semi-intensive systems based on pasture where animals can be up to 20 months of age at slaughter. The British countryside is full of public footpaths and pedestrian right-of-ways and there is enough trouble with ramblers on this account with breeding bulls without having fields of fattening bulls as an additional hazard or bone of contention. Yard finishing of bulls over 12 months would be safer (except possibly for the stockmen) but here there is another drawback, namely excessive sexual activity which is bound to affect efficiency of food use. It does not seem that bull beef has much future in Britain with production systems that are mainly dependent on grazing and conserved fodder.

The implantation or oral administration of synthetic steroids is an American innovation of the early fifties and the practice is widespread with feed-lot finishing in that country, but it is less common in Britain. Tests have established that there is up to 16 per cent increase in the growth rate of steers on high cereal diets as a result of implantation and, as a further bonus, up to 10 per cent gain in feed efficiency. Implantations appear to be much less effective with cattle at pasture. Synthetic oestrogens are not recommended for heifers because of side effects, in particular increased mammary development and, in extreme cases, vaginal prolapse but these are much less evident with the oral administration of synthetic progesterones which are akin to the birth control pill in humans. Their effect is to suppress oestrus and to boost growth rates by up to 10 per cent.

Apart from any boost in growth rate hormone administration increases the proportion of lean meat in the carcass at the expense of fat. There has been some buyer discrimination against treated steers because of side effects and in some countries, notably France, Italy and Sweden, there is a ban on the use of hormones because of suspected carcinogenic effects. Normally hormones are withdrawn from feed at least two days before slaughter and in the case of implants any residue is discarded with the ears. With these precautions it is doubtful whether any residue could be detected in a beef carcass but nevertheless they are not favoured in Britain.

PRODUCTION OF SUCKLED CALVES

The production of calves, specially bred for beef, which suckle their dams for up to nine months, is biologically an inefficient operation and it is not appropriate to an agriculture where there is a heavy pressure on land, which is the case in most countries of Western Europe. It is a different matter in New World countries where land is relatively plentiful and individual holdings are big enough to give farmers a reasonable living without pressures to substitute more intensive enterprises. Western European countries do not have the big open spaces of Argentina or the western rangelands of the United States and so they have to put a main reliance on their dairy industries for domestic beef and veal production. Because of this they tend to favour dual-purpose breeds such as Dutch and German Friesians and the Brown Swiss.

Britain is something of an exception among Western European countries in that, despite a recent decline, there are still over a million cows kept solely for the production of beef. There are several reasons for this and some of them have a historical basis. For instance when Britain's economy depended largely on the export of goods and services and the importation of food and raw materials, in what was essentially a free trade situation up till 1939, a great deal of British agriculture went into a decline which resulted in a lot of the poorer quality land, that had formerly been in crops, being returned to grass. A combination of ewes and beef cows in low input systems was a logical solution. Generally the structure of British farming, in particular the greater unit size and the relative freedom from fragmentation, fitted them to more extensive forms of farming than those practised in Continental countries which for the most part have had agriculture that has been heavily protected.

The plough-up policy of the nineteen-forties had its effect on beef as well as sheep production and both branches of farming went into a decline. This was reversed in the beef sector in the early fifties as a result of a political promise to increase the availability of 'red meat' that had suffered largely as a consequence of declining exports from the Argentine. Apart from attractive guaranteed prices for beef which seemed to enjoy a handsome boost at every succeeding Price Review, there were headage subsidies, one awarded at the 9-month

stage for animals ajudged to be of suitable conformation for
beef and another, applicable in the first instance to what was
adjudged to be hill land, for breeding cows producing beef
calves. Later, the latter subsidy was extended, at a half rate, to
cover lowland cows.

There followed a rapid expansioin of the national beef
breeding herd. Hardy breeds like the Galloway and Welsh
Black and later the Luing and crosses such as the Blue Grey
(White Shorthorn × Galloway) and the Cross Highland
(Shorthorn × Highland) according to the local preference were
favoured on the harder hills. On lower land though the so-
called Irish cow, bred from a Dairy Shorthorn cow and sired
either by an Aberdeen Angus or Hereford bull, has been very
popular and for very good reasons. As it is hand-reared it is
docile and very tractable which are important traits, particularly when one is handling stock at calving time. It has plenty
of frame and a reasonable flow of milk and generally it
produces a very good weaner. The supply of heifers of this
breeding are declining with the continuing replacement of the
Dairy Shorthorn by the Friesian in Ireland, and Angus or
Hereford crosses by the Friesian, either local or imported from
Ireland, have of necessity taken over from the original Irish
heifer. There are complaints that these can have too much milk
but this criticism is less valid with autumn calving and a winter
diet of silage particularly with Charolais or Simmental calves,
which have the frame to benefit from the extra milk when its
flow freshens in response to spring grass.

The headage subsidies were indiscriminate inasmuch as
there was no additional reward for extra quality in stock, apart
from that subsequently earned in the sale ring. Subsidies could
account for as much as a third of the total realisations from
cattle on a hill farm and so numbers took precedence over
quality. The situation has been largely corrected with reduced
subsidies and as a result breeders are paying much more attention to calf quality, particularly in respect of growth potential.
This is reflected in the spectacular rise in the popularity

of the larger imported breeds, notably the Charolais, as a terminal sire at the expense of domestic breeds, even on hill farms.

Nowhere is this upsurge in the quality of suckled calves, in respect of feeders requirements, seen to better effect than in the Borders which is a region of large farms with a long-established livestock tradition. As recently as the early sixties the favoured terminal sire was the Aberdeen Angus with its fully-justified reputation for quality beef. However it was then in the process of being superseded by the Hereford because of this breed's better growth performance. The sad fact was that Aberdeen Angus breeders were paying the penalty of subscribing to the standard of the export market which required a compact type rather than the needs of the domestic feeder who required animals that did not get excessively fat at light weights. Before the Hereford could achieve any marked dominance the Charolais came on to the scene first via artificial insemination and then, as the breed became established in Britain and the price of bulls fell to commercially realistic levels, with natural service. Now on either side of the Tweed for a distance of fifty miles one seldom sees feeding cattle (other than dairy-bred stores) either in yards or on pastures that are not sired by one of the imported breeds and, among these, the Charolais occupies number one place.

There are some criticisms of the Charolais, particularly in respect of difficult calvings but these can be kept to acceptable levels partly by choice of bull but mainly by having breeding cows in very moderate condition at calving. This will reduce birth weights and assisted calvings, and lessen the risk of calf mortalities. Some breeders have had so much trouble with the Charolais that they have switched to the Simmental or the Limousin which of the imported breeds is the safest for mating to maiden heifers. Though it does not have the growth of the Charolais it produces what is generally agreed to be the best quality carcass from a butcher's viewpoint of all the imported breeds and it promises to have a rosy future in Britain.

Another change in the industry has been the trend from spring to back-end calving which in some respects goes against logic for early spring is the natural time for calving and it also gives the best match between the availability of grazing and the nutritional needs of the cows. But there are other factors that have to be taken into consideration and of these the sale value of weaners is paramount. As explained in a previous section the autumn-born calf will, barring accidents, finish in its second winter and the feeder is able to turn over his investment and hopefully make a profit in a matter of a few months. The purchaser of the March- or April-born calves has to wait for up to twelve months before he can realise his investment if he carries them through to the finishing stage. Another argument, particularly potent when the elements are often at their most vindictive in the early spring, is that generally weather conditions are more favourable for newly-dropped calves in the autumn.

Regardless of month of calving most stockmen prefer to keep cows and calves outside until the latter are at least a month old at which time the calves have acquired some resistance to white scours which can be a serious problem with indoor calving. Some form of housing usually becomes essential especially when autumn calving with completion of pasture improvement programmes. Poaching of a rough pasture is one thing but it can spell the ruination of a good sward. Out-wintered cows have often been used as tools in the reclamation of moorland for treading has helped to break up the peat layer and exposed mineral soil while dung and urine have increased fertility, but eventually a point is reached where out-wintering does more harm than good and housing becomes a necessity to protect subsequent spring growth. Needless to say it must be cheap housing, and a simple kennel arrangement with a covered creep area for calves is normally adequate. Possibly the greatest hazard apart from calf scours that the calf breeder has to face is hypomagnesaemia which is discussed at some length in Chapter 6.

Prevention is based on some form of supplementation which gives a daily intake of about 50–60 gm of calcined magnesite over periods of risk. This can take the form of fortified home mixes of trough food, proprietary high-magnesium pencils or sprinkling magnesite on silage where this is a main feed. Some farmers favour the use of dolomitic limestone on pastures but this will do no good if there is nothing to graze and this is often when the problem is encountered. In this situation it is a misnomer to label the disease grass staggers.

A major difficulty of autumn-calving that must if possible be countered is a gradual regression to spring calving with its attendant management difficulties and a loss of uniformity in the annual crop of weaners. An important factor in determining conception is condition of cows at mating. If they are in a negative balance conception rates are poor, so it is important to have them gaining weight from about two months after calving. With a deliberate policy of restricted feeding towards the end of pregnancy and the inevitable milking off of body reserves early in lactation positive steps must be taken to prevent any further loss of condition.

One of the major advantages claimed for back-end calving is the greater appetite of calves during the height of the growing season as compared with younger spring-born calves. Also, if there is any shortage of grass due to summer drought, they can be weaned and given preferential treatment in respect of grazing but normally they will remain on their mothers until at least 6–8 weeks before the next due date. It is important not to lose bloom when there is a period between weaning and sale or, in the case of home finishers, the beginning of the winter feeding regime. Having regard to the declining quality of autumn grass, supplementation with rolled barley often with as little as 1–2 kg/day is advisable. There is no need to include a protein additive because there is ample protein in autumn grass. One must always remember that the production of suckled calves must essentially be a low-cost operation if it is to return a profit.

Chapter 18

MILK FROM GRASS

Milk production carried out reasonably well, will in most circumstances produce the highest returns per hectare of grassland compared with any other grazing livestock system. Over the years many different systems of milk production have evolved, employing grazed grass and conserved grass products together with other feed inputs in varying proportions. In this book we are concerned with both the proportion of milk produced from grass and more importantly the actual quantity of milk produced per hectare of grassland.

It is very difficult to compare two farms in terms of their efficiency. On the one hand we have milk producers who get virtually all their production from bought concentrates, and merely use their pastures for little more than maintenance and exercise. On the other hand we have the grassland fanatic who firmly believes that grass in late September will support a cow producing 22 litres per day, while retaining sufficient condition on her back to enable her to get in calf again.

These are extreme examples, both of which have been caught on the band wagon current at one time or another, and have never been able, or have had any desire to get off it. However, the point that we would like to make is that the middle of the road is often the wisest course. The sensible use of concentrates, with good grazing and conservation management, and an intelligent use of fertilisers, is the way to reasonable profits from the dairy herd.

When looking at a dairying enterprise, there are so many variables that can result in a similar margin per cow or per hectare that we have to be very careful to note how the milk producer arrives at the figures that he quotes. High margins per cow with low stocking rates may correspond in margin per hectare with low margins per cow but a very high stocking rate.

With the continued increase in cow values, land and buildings, it is inevitable that there is a threshold below which production per cow must not fall. This will of course vary with the current variable costs of the dairy enterprise, and in particular the fixed costs situation of a farm, particularly after a large capital injection in the provision of buildings or with a newly-acquired farm carrying a high rental equivalent in the form of interest payments. At present a minimum of 5,000 litres per Friesian cow per year is necessary with all systems, other than a few farms blessed with abnormally low fixed costs.

CONCENTRATES – HOW MUCH?

The most important question that an open-minded milk producer must answer is: 'What level of concentrates can I use to give me the most profitable system?' or conversely, 'How much reliance do I place on grazed and conserved grass?' Does he aim for 7,500 litres produced per cow per annum using 2,500 kg of concentrate feed or 4,500 litres with 1,500 kg of concentrates? Both these systems rely on concentrate usage of 0·35 kg per litre which is still below the average for concentrate usage throughout the United Kingdom. With present milk and concentrate prices, and this has been true for a very long time, the former is better off financially than the latter. Unfortunately, there are too many farmers who record the higher level of concentrate use and the lower level of milk production, largely because both their herd and their pasture management are deficient.

In many respects milk production per hectare is a much more satisfactory economic criterion than production per cow. It will be remembered from Chapter 7 that New Zealand evidence, obtained by direct experiment as well as from farm surveys, proves conclusively that rate of stocking is a more important factor in determining level of yield per hectare than is production per cow, up to a certain critical point where reduced yields per cow through over-stocking are not compensated by the greater stock density.

The Milk Marketing Board of England and Wales, Farm Management Services data for the year 1981–2 also show very clearly the effect of stocking rate. Gross margin increased rapidly from £491 per hectare for the 218 farms recorded with a stocking rate below 1·60 cows per hectare (average 1·38 cows/hectare) to £1,300 per hectare for the 35 herds with the very high stocking rate of over 3·00 cows per hectare (average 3·38 cows/hectare) in their sample of 1,130 costed herds.

It is interesting and important to note that the highest level of stocking had no detrimental effect on yield per cow, as would have been expected a few years ago. The 35 herds averaged 5,338 litres per cow while the much lower stocked 218 herds averaged only 5,040 litres per cow. This was not due to substitution of acres by concentrated feed, as the total usage of concentrates was very similar being 1,873 kg (0·35 kg/litre) in the former and 1,713 kg (0·34 kg/litre) on the latter farms. This evidence shows that intensity of stocking is a major factor in determining both level of production and normally the level of profitability per hectare under British conditions.

Contrary to prediction, the response of a higher yield per cow as well as, of course, per hectare, with a higher stocking rate is very interesting. As the farm gets more 'tuned up' with an increase in stocking rate, both grassland management and conservation of grass for winter have to be excellent. Timeliness is very important and mistakes cannot be made otherwise the results, both physical and financial, will be seriously affected. It is these farms that are often most vulnerable to adverse weather conditions, either drought or excessively wet or cold periods, compared with lower stocked farms where there is sufficient 'slack' to withstand these periods. On highly-stocked farms management decisions must be right, examples of this are that silage-making cannot be 'left for another week' or the application of fertiliser nitrogen to grazing fields delayed. With the former a decrease in 'D' value by three points can seriously effect planned winter production or increase concentrate usage; at the same time the delay slows down the growth of the much-needed regrowth to satisfy the grazing programme. Five days delay in applying fertiliser nitrogen 'over the Bank Holiday' does not seem a long time but that nitrogen is needed by the growing sward. Four days is in fact 2 per cent of the 200-day growing season. Two per cent reduction in grassland production per year means two less cows in a 100-cow herd. A quick calculation at 1983 prices will result in a £1,800 loss of milk sales per annum alone!

The psychological reaction is that the greater the concentration of stock on the farm, the greater the progressive farmers' effort to grow more feed and to utilise it efficiently. Provided these things are done sensibly, further economies will come through a better spread of overheads and a higher output per labour unit.

GRAZING METHODS

Accepting that a high density of stocking is an important factor in determining profit per hectare, we turn now to the problem of ensuring that this is achieved within safe limits. The main factors here are the level of production of grass nutrients, their quality, and the system of grazing. The point was established in Chapter 7 that some form of controlled grazing, whether it be by the use of the fold electric fence or by close semi-permanent subdivision to permit paddock-grazing, introduces a critical element of budgeting into the planning of food supplies. It gives opportunities for discreet management of portions of the grazing area, and it reduces the danger of feast and famine, a critically important consideration under our conditions because a farmer can build up food reserves in the form of hay and silage to the point where he has confidence in increasing stocking rate.

If he wishes to increase output even more he can then move from a reliance on clover nitrogen to fertiliser nitrogen, provided he has the additional stock to make good use of this additional herbage. Thus, unlike his New Zealand counterpart, who is denied the use of concentrates on economic grounds, he has another tool which, used sensibly, can further assist his efforts to achieve economies of scale.

In the last few years the current 'fashionable' system of grazing has changed dramatically. The electric fence with daily or twice-daily moves as strips or fold-grazing gave way to a paddock system with numerous subdivisions of fields, with probably twenty-one paddocks being the most popular. Within a short time, however, we were back to a set-stocking type of system, allowing the dairy herd to graze a large area unhindered by subdivisions. The new system of set stocking was, however, very different from that practised before the advent of the electric fence, with the use of better swards and in most instances a much higher use of nitrogen fertiliser comparable to fold or paddock-grazing systems, and is usually applied at three-weekly or monthly intervals in all three systems. The results obtained from these grazing systems in terms of production per hectare is very similar provided the sward is good, the cows are good, the overall management is good, and that similar levels of nitrogen fertiliser are used at whatever level. Differences in results between farms with similar basic raw material being almost entirely due to the management ability of the operations involved.

ADVANTAGES AND DISADVANTAGES OF GRAZING SYSTEMS

What are the advantages and disadvantages of each of these three systems? Daily moving of the electric fence is still a good system and there are signs that this system is returning to many farms, provided the person who moves the fence is in sympathy with the herd and can therefore be relied upon to move the fence the correct distance. The only person really qualified to do this, or to issue instructions, is the man who milks the cows. He will be able to detect small differences in daily yield if insufficient grass is provided, and it is this monitor, plus refusals or over-grazing that he must bear in mind. This system has many merits, the most important being that there is control and in fact what is produced is a series of paddocks, the size of which is related to grass growth.

As with paddock-grazing, however, a thin line of electrified wire provides little shelter for a cow, and there is often no place to seek shelter in rough weather. The provision of a back fence is a further refinement, whereby grazing is confined to the day's area only. Cows cannot return to the area grazed previously, and this allows for uninterrupted regrowth. Damage to the pasture by repeated regrazing of the young regrowth and treading by the herd are avoided, as these are responsible for weakening the grass plant and reducing production.

A major disadvantage of the system is the time it takes to move the fence once or twice daily and frequently the moving of the whole fence between fields. Also the high concentration of stock in a small area can result in severe poaching in bad weather.

The initial cost of setting up a paddock system is high as well as the provision of water at a place that involves the minimum of walking. Cows will not walk far for water – a shortage affects yields and water is cheaper than milk. The main advantage of a paddock system after it is set up is the very low labour input needed with a change daily between paddocks. For the purist, however, the main objection to the system is that a fixed number of paddocks are involved, and subject to minor deviations cows return after a fixed period to each paddock, that is every 21 days in a 21-paddock system. The rate of grass growth, however, is not constant throughout the growing season, and in May for example 14–16 days is a sufficient period between grazings, while in a dry period in July or August

21 days' regrowth in a paddock is insufficient for the herd. Management of the system can however take care of these fluctuations in rate of growth. In May a few paddocks can be left for silage, and in August part of the conservation area may be used for grazing. In August, however, with an autumn-calving herd in particular, the need for grass is reduced in late lactation, or as often happens, dry cows are removed from the main herd and grazed separately. The problem of surplus grass for silage is fairly easily overcome by clearing the surplus paddocks for silage, and if the area involved does not fit into the normal pattern of silage-making, the new technique of making 'big bale' silage is a very useful way of conserving a relatively small area when the quantity involved does not justify opening the main silage pit.

There is no doubt that a paddock-grazing system has served and is still serving its purpose well on many dairy farms. It introduced a discipline whereby within limits the farmer knew his grazing programme well in advance, and the discipline of having a planned system gave him confidence to increase his stocking rate to a more profitable level. The system ensured the timely application of fertiliser, and also made sure that as a planned proportion of the farm had been laid up for conservation, and unless a disaster such as drought or cold and wet weather prevented grass growth, he would be fairly sure of an adequate planned tonnage of silage at the beginning of the winter.

Before the dairy industry had really settled down to the disciplines of paddock-grazing, the dairy farmer was confronted with yet another system of grazing, previously associated with beef cattle and sheep enterprises. Set-stocking allows a given area for the whole herd for grazing, this area depending on soil type, class of land, size of cow and of course nitrogen fertiliser usage. It was argued that continuous set-stocking helped to produce a ley with a great density of tillers, the thick sward not being as open as that produced by a system of rotational grazing, where continued growing, followed by defoliation, caused the base of the sward to open. A sward is grazed at the vigorously growing stage with a high nutritive value. It is also, contrary to prediction, able to sustain a high stocking rate and production of milk similar to other systems with a comparable management input. With this system the provision of water is relatively easy and also with the larger area involved at any one time, on most farms there will be part of the area that will provide shelter for the herd.

The collecting of the herd in early morning in particular has been solved by subdividing the area for day and night grazing, the night area or areas being closer to the steading.

In practice it has been found that provided they are well managed each of the systems of grazing results in very similar outputs per acre. As always it is the person in charge who has the greatest effect on production, whatever system of grazing is employed.

When discussing grazing we must remember that we are dealing with a whole-farm situation. A dairy herd kept on a mainly arable farm, where short-term leys are used for part at least of the grazing area, will not justify an expensive paddock system which will have to be removed at the end of one grazing season. The provision of grass for conservation is also an important factor. An intensively grazed ley will become progressively more fouled with dung pats, although on the other hand, after a few years of heavy stocking, a state where the build-up of micro-organisms and earthworm activity is so great that dung pats disappear very quickly, thus easing the fouling problem. On many farms this fouling is quite simply overcome by integrating cutting and grazing when this is possible. A field may be grazed once or twice in spring, shut up for a cut of grass for silage, and returns to the grazing system as palatable regrowth.

We do not want to create the impression that all milk producers use paddocks or strip grazing methods. Herds in arable areas with short leys cannot justify the expense of setting up a paddock system for one year and it is under these circumstances that an intelligent application of fold-grazing can pay dividends. Many herds, however, graze a field for 4–5 days before moving on to the next. This has a serious disadvantage in that the cows have a progressive deterioration in the quality of their grazing with a consequent fluctuation in milk yields.

There is a considerable danger when a large field is fold-grazed that the last breaks may suffer deterioration with an opening up of the sward and loss of clover, caused by grazing at a very advanced stage of growth and consequent overshading effects. This will often occur when fold-grazing of a field is repeated several times in succession in the one season. Because shading of clover is more likely early in the season there is much to be said for fairly lax strip grazing at this time in order to go over a field fairly quickly.

There is another sound reason for adopting this procedure, especially in districts where cold spells of weather are common-place in the spring. If a pasture has attained some length and is grazed very bare, the onset of unfavourable weather conditions will result in very poor recovery, but if some leaf is left after grazing the pasture keeps growing. In order to counter the ill-effects of fouling by this rather extensive form of grazing, such pastures are closed after two visits by the herd for late-spring silage at a time when clover is better able to compete with grass than it is earlier in the year. Under this system, the electric fence comes into its own from about the beginning of May, when most fields are closed for conservation and when grass growth is rapid.

Invariably the pastures which bear the brunt of fold-grazing during May and June open up to some extent, and by the beginning of July they will carry some rough patches which are largely the result of fouling. Sometimes such fields are closed for a light crop of late hay or silage, or else they are hard grazed by the ewe flock after weaning. The autumn flush, needless to say, is rationed carefully with the electric fence to avoid wastage.

At Cockle Park we were fortunate in having sheep in conjunction with dairying, because they are so useful in combating any opening-up effects in the sward due to the grazing by dairy cows. Generally, if a sward becomes open and there is loss of clover, often aggravated by a fairly heavy use of nitrogen, it will become a fat lamb pasture for a year. This has a further advantage so far as the lambs are concerned, in that one is certain that they are on clean pasture.

Farmers who have no sheep and do not practise a strict two-sward system can at least use the mowing machine to keep their pastures fresh and and in active growth. Wherever intensive stocking is practised an endeavour should be made to alternate grazing and mowing, in so far as this is practicable. However, mowing should also be part of the conservation plan, so that two purposes are served, and this plan should be formulated early in the year. One or more fields which are not grazed at the beginning of the season are harvested as the first silage to be made and, cut at the flag stage, these will produce a good aftermath which will come into the grazing rotation as fields that have been grazed more than once are laid up for conservation and cleaning.

There may have to be deviations from the original plan as the season progresses. More or less grass may be conserved than was originally intended, but the overall aim must be to avoid any waste of grass or of its growth potential so that adequate reserves of winter fodder are created. Anyone who wishes to expand output cannot have too much silage or hay. Once this point is reached, upward adjustments in stocking can be made with confidence because the feeding prospect is secure for the future.

STOCKING POLICY

What is a reasonable concentration of stock on a mainly grassland dairy farm? No firm answer can be made to this question, because of variations in climate, soil, and fertiliser practice. On good deep soil, however, with a satisfactory rainfall distribution (or with irrigation), it is now reasonable to aim at a cow equivalent to 0·4 hectare of grassland and forage crop, with not more than 1·5 tonnes of homegrown or purchased concentrates per cow equivalent, unless yields per cow are appreciably above average. A cow equivalent is defined as any animal that enters the milking herd, or any two animals in the process of rearing, excluding calves under three months, which are still on milk or mainly purchased food.

It is important to keep rearing stock to a minimum, especially on the smaller farm, because they are maintained largely at the expense of milking cows, which make a more remunerative use of food. This reflects the importance of calving heifers for the first time at an early age, certainly not later than 2½ years, and of maintaining a high proportion of mature cows in the herd. These are points of general farm management rather than grassland management, but nevertheless they are very important in securing maximum profit from grassland.

RATIONING OF CONCENTRATES

Returning again to the question of levels of concentrate feeding, where there is a main reliance on pasture we prefer not to think in terms of getting maintenance and x litres from grass or bulk foods and feeding concentrates for y litres. This is partly because the practice makes a distinction between nutrients from different sources which a cow's metabolism does not necessarily recognise, and partly because it does not emphasise sufficiently the economic significance of level of concentrate feeding in relation to yield.

For example, if one is told that a Friesian herd is averaging 25 litres of milk daily with the use of 0·35 kg of concentrates per litre during the winter months, there is the knowledge that reasonable standards are being achieved. If, however, the performance falls appreciably below this standard, one should start to examine the management factors responsible for the decline. Possibly there are too many stale cows as a result of a bad calving pattern; yields may be suffering from poor milking methods; or, most important in this context, there may be insufficient quality in the hay and silage. A simple statement of average yield and concentrate use for given periods becomes very valuable in management when one has records over a succession of years. It gives a basis for critical assessment, not only of progress or otherwise, but of management factors influencing the situation.

There is another argument against the maintenance-plus approach to the feeding of dairy cows. One may send a sample of silage away for analysis and get a report back indicating a good enough feed for maintenance and the first 10 litres. When a cow's yield approximates to this level of production and her concentrate ration is suddenly cut off there will be a sharp fall in her production. This will be due primarily to a change in her management. It should not be interpreted that the silage is necessarily below the value stated and that there must be a general raising of concentrate feeding to all cows.

Except where cows have reached the point of drying off, it is almost better where one is relying largely on bulk foods in the winter to think in terms of feeding say 0·2 kg of concentrate/ litre to the cow giving 10 litres, 0·25 kg for the cow giving 15 litres, and so on up to a maximum of 0·45 kg per litre for the cow giving 35 litres or more. This is a different approach from the conventional one, but it is rather more appropriate to the farm where a conscientious effort is being made to provide good hay and silage, and when there is a high level of herd management.

It may be possible if the bulks are of exceptional quality to provide lower rates of concentrate feeding or it may be necessary to raise them a little if the bulks are not up to standard. In fact, a farmer is advised to experiment a little on his own behalf when he starts a clamp of silage to see what level of concentrate feeding he should be following, using the cows that have settled down in their lactations.

Differential feeding of concentrates in this rather precise manner may be a little complicated for the large herd which is handled by a small labour force. Here a farmer may elect to feed a flat rate per litre for all cows giving 7 litres of milk or more during the winter months, the rate per litre being varied each year according to the quality of silage and hay available. The quality of the herd and the herd management would also influence this decision, inasmuch as a man with a management herd potential of 6,000 litres per cow would be justified in feeding a much higher rate than the man with a 4,500 litre level of herd and management.

Such a flat rate of feeding does not cater for the exceptional cow that is unable to manage a large intake of bulk foods. But this sort of farmer is less interested in the individual performance than he is in the average performance of his herd, although he must always be looking critically at his results in relation to rising costs.

The greatest economies in concentrate use can be made in the grazing part of the dairying year, especially from May on to the start of autumn calving. It is not suggested that there should be a sudden cutting off of concentrates when cows go out to early grass, as this may be positively dangerous because of grass tetany or staggers. Wherever there is a risk of this, it is advisable to continue feeding some concentrates fortified with calcined magnesite to all cows giving 15 litres or more daily, say at the rate of 0·2 kg per litre until the feed hardens in early May. This need be no more than a grain or dried sugar beet supplement, because excepting the really high yielder, any cow getting a belly full of spring grass twice a day will be receiving all the protein she needs. Economies can be made not only by feeding less concentrates but by substituting cheap starchy foods for expensive protein when there is ample grass protein in the diet.

A question left unanswered is what one does with a 35-litre

spring calver on grass in May. Our answer is to feed cereals after 25 litres at some 0·5 kg per litre.

In our experience, two things may happen if this cow is not fed. Firstly the cow will lose flesh rapidly and consequently will be extremely difficult to get in calf while she is losing weight, and secondly she will rapidly come down from her peak yield and often settle at some 18–20 litres, in fact, lower than a herd mate who may have peaked at only 25 litres per day.

We have, however, a high regard for the adequacy of spring and summer grass for cows that have been in milk for five months or more, but the value of autumn grass can be over-estimated, especially for freshly-calved cows. These may be milking well at the outset of lactation but largely because they are milking off condition. Once a cow loses condition and falls sharply in her production at this time of the year, no amount of subsequent good feeding will restore the level of yield. It is better to think of autumn grass for this category of cow as one thinks of good silage later in the year, and feed accordingly. It is a different matter, of course, with a late-winter calver which is nearing the end of her lactation, for it is unlikely that worthwhile response will be obtained from concentrates if the autumn grass is of reasonable quality.

Chapter 19

SUMMER OR WINTER MILK PRODUCTION?

CONTRASTS BETWEEN BRITAIN AND NEW ZEALAND

The majority of British dairy farmers aim to calve their cows in the autumn to take advantage of the higher prices that have prevailed for milk during the winter months. This pricing policy has been dictated by the need to ensure that there are adequate supplies for the lucrative liquid milk market as opposed to the less remunerative outlets such as cheese and butter manufacture which have had to compete with cheap sources of supply, either the highly subsidised countries of Western Europe or such a country as New Zealand where the natural and economic conditions make it possible to produce manufacturing milk very cheaply. The New Zealand dairy farmer would count himself very fortunate if he were getting as much as half the price that his British counterpart has been receiving in recent years.

Calving on a typical New Zealand factory-supply farm starts just prior to the onset of active pasture growth, for experience has shown that this pattern of calving results in the cheapest and most efficient systems of production under New Zealand conditions. The great majority of the dairy farms are family concerns and it is common for no more than two people to look after herds of 100–150 cows and do all the other work associated with the running of a farm. It is understandable therefore that farmers aim to develop a system that not only minimises labour effort, but also gives them a break of at least two months from the twice-daily chore of milking cows.

They secure this objective by seasonal production. Through calving in the early spring they ensure that the peak nutritional demands of the herd in the four-month period after calving coincide with a period when grass is at its best, nutritionally. As pasture starts to fail both qualitatively and quantitatively in the autumn, the herd is approaching the drying-off stage. There is a relatively long dry period of at least sixty days when the herd will be maintained on hay or silage, which is essentially a by-product of the intensive grazing management practised during the main growing season. There is nothing like the same emphasis placed on the quality of conserved grass that one finds on the better grassland dairy farms in Britain which have to cater for the winter needs of herds that are at a peak potential for milk production.

There is a big emphasis on stocking intensity and most of the better New Zealand dairy farms will carry a cow equivalent or higher to 0·4 hectare, without any purchased food. Much more weight is placed on yield per hectare than on yield per cow. In other words, in order to maximise utilisation of pasture, farmers accept a reduction in yield per cow as a consequence of high stocking rates, provided their overall objective of high production per unit area is achieved. Even with this, because of good cows and good stockmanship, it is not uncommon to find herds of Friesian and Friesian-cross cows which will average 4,000 litres of milk or more, testing over 4 per cent of butterfat. Naturally yields per cow are much lower in Jersey herds, but yields per hectare are only slightly less than those achieved by Friesian herds because of the higher stocking intensities that are possible with the smaller breed. There are many dairy farms in New Zealand that produce more than 9,000 litres of milk per forage hectare, which is almost entirely grassland, and rear all replacement stock into the bargain.

The New Zealand approach to pastoral dairy farming, with its emphasis on utilisation *in situ* and a very different calving pattern, is in marked contrast to that in Britain where the majority of cows are on diets that are strongly fortified by concentrates in the winter months when they are in full milk. When they go out to pasture they are mainly stale cows and though there is usually a lift in daily yields it is only rarely that autumn-calving cows will average appreciably more than 25 litres per day when they are out at grass. The calving peak is not so distinct as it is in New Zealand. Though most farmers calve their replacement heifers in the early autumn, inevitably there is a slip back in calving dates. Heat periods are of a relatively short duration in the winter months, especially where nutrition is inadequate, and it is not surprising that herdsmen often fail to observe that cows are in season. The inevitable consequence is that most of the so-called autumn-calving herds have a calving spread that extends from the late summer to the late winter and as a result dairymen are milking cows every day of the year.

In contrast, the typical New Zealand factory supply herd has a calving spread of no more than 6–7 weeks. This is not achieved by heavy culling because annual herd wastage from all causes – low production, failure to breed, disease and accidents – is below 20 per cent. The simple fact is that it is easier to get cows in calf in the early summer than it is at any other time of the year and there is seldom any difficulty in determining which cows are in season when they are out at pasture and they are being mounted by other cows.

SUMMER MILK PRODUCTION AT COCKLE PARK

It is not surprising that the senior author, with his New Zealand background and a feeling of certainty that Britain would be in the Common Market before many years were out, turned his thoughts about the mid-nineteen sixties to the possibilities of developing a milk production unit at Cockle Park that was very much on the New Zealand pattern. He argued that if there was going to be Common Market prices for butter and cheese, which are both storable commodities, and also Common Market costs for concentrates, it would be better for Britain that the highest possible proportion of manufacturing milk should be produced cheaply from grass as grazing, rather than from conserved grass that has to be supplemented with expensive concentrates.

Cockle Park, with its cold heavy soils and late springs, is in one of the less favoured parts of Britain for summer milk production but it was felt that if the project succeeded there the point would be made for other regions of Britain notably the west and south-west, where the growing season is much longer and it is possible for herds to have reasonably good grazing for up to nine months in the year.

The unit was established in 1969, mainly with a herd of two-year-old Jersey heifers. By 1972 a more normal age balance was achieved in the herd of 48 cows which was run on a block of 15 hectares of which 3 hectares was in barley undersown with RvP ryegrass for the 1973 grazing season. The remaining 12 hectare were all in ryegrass and these supplied the grazing needs of the herd as well as 180 tonnes of wilted silage for winter feeding. The 3 hectares of barley were not sufficient for the total cereal needs for the herd and so a small quantity of barley had to be bought in from the main farm. The only other purchased food was high magnesium pencils which were fed as a precautionary measure against hypomagnesaemia until about the end of May. The barley straw, with an appreciable amount of Italian ryegrass in it, is a valuable source of additional nutriment for the cows just after they are dried off.

In 1972, the last year of this project, a stocking rate of a cow to 0·25 hectare of grass was maintained throughout the season and the concentrates usage per litre (almost entirely barley) was 0·77 kg. The yield per grassland hectare was 11,900 litres as compared with 11,700 litres in 1971. Comparatively, 1972 was a much poorer grass year with a late, cold spring, a lot of early summer poaching, and drought from the beginning of August to November. As a consequence of a foreshortened lactation averaging 270 days, milk yielded at 2,950 litres per cow, was appreciably lower than one can expect even with such stocking rates in a normal season. The target figure was in fact 3,200 litres per cow which was a reasonable expectation for an age-balanced herd of Jerseys, that had been subjected to selection, under these conditions.

Nevertheless the financial results in 1972, taking into account the then current returns for dairying, were impressive with a gross margin of £524 per grass hectare and £405 per forage hectare. This last figure was obtained by adding to the total area of the unit, the acreage equivalent of the 'purchased' barley. These margins were nearly double the normal returns at that time.

FRONDEG FARM IN CARDIGANSHIRE

Not to be outdone by Cockle Park, the junior author, when the Welsh Agricultural College took possession in 1970 of Frondeg Farm, decided to make summer milk production the main enterprise. He chose Friesians and he had more than a personal attachment to the breed to justify his choice because, the need in Britain is for dual-purpose cows even if the quality of their milk for manufacturing purposes is not all that is desired. By 1983 the farm of 56 hectares was carrying 120 milking cows and 66 head of replacement stock and also providing winter grazing for 250 breeding ewes. The herd now averages 6,000 litres with a concentrate usage of 0·31 kg per litre and a stocking rate of 2·56 cows per hectare giving a margin over feed and fertiliser per hectare of £1,454.

After 12 years this farm is still very much in the process of development. The herd is still relatively young and there has not been as yet an opportunity to select cows as many in the herd are in the category of make-weights until such time as they can be replaced by stock of greater potential. The fertility level of the farm was initially very low and in our experience, no matter how liberal one is with lime, phosphate, potash and nitrogen at the beginning, it takes several years before pasture land is brought into full heart. Both Stapledon and Levy, the high priests of grassland farming in Britain and New Zealand respectively, stressed the importance of 'stock fertility'. This implies the build-up of the biological component of soils as a result of producing more grass and carrying more stock, with an enhanced return of excrements that add to biological activity in the soil. This has never been properly defined but it is a very real phenomenon. One has only to see New Zealand grassland farms that have doubled and trebled in carrying capacity over the years to appreciate the dynamics of grassland improvement which cannot be accounted for by the fertility status of soils, when expressed purely in terms of conventional chemical analysis of plant nutrients.

SUMMER MILK PRODUCTION

Summer milk production has its problems; for instance, there is a suspicion that the feeding of magnesite to combat the dangers of hypomagnesaemia in the spring impairs conception, and it is possible that here is a veterinary problem yet to be resolved.

Again we can be by no means certain about the levels or the duration of concentrate feeding that should be adopted to get the most economic response. The weight of experimental evidence relating to cows fed concentrates when they are on good grass indicates that for the duration of the trials, the response to concentrate feeding is insufficient to justify its use. Some years ago Dr Don McClusky, while he was at Newcastle, reviewed both Dutch and British literature and came to the conclusion, after examining the results of more than thirty trials, that it took on average 3 kg of concentrates to produce an extra litre of milk as compared with cows that were full-fed on grass alone.

However, these results referred to the duration of the experiment and average cows. They took no account of freshly-calved cows which, when fully fed, were capable of producing 35–40 litres per day; the residual effects of good feeding early in lactation on yields later in lactation; nor the ups and downs of pasture production under farm conditions. It has been well-established that peak yield, provided it is accompanied by adequate nutrition subsequent to this peak, has a marked influence on the total yield for a lactation. Expressed in another way, an identical twin with a low peak yield as a consequence of inadequate feeding prior to and subsequent to calving will not in later stages of lactation match the level of production of its twin mate that has had a higher level of nutrition at these critical times, even when they are subsequently given the same level of nutrition. Just as the child is father to the man, so then does feeding of a cow before and after calving have a profound effect on total performance during the subsequent lactation.

It is possible, too, that there is an important individual cow reaction to a complete reliance on pastures inasmuch as some cows may be superior to others in making the best of the grass that is offered them. There was more than a hint of this in the observations Hancock made at Ruakura in New Zealand on the grazing habits of identical twins. High-yielding twin pairs characteristically spent a longer time grazing than low-yielding pairs and were more selective in the grass they ate. In that country, where there has been selection for high yields with pasture feeding over many generations, it is not uncommon for Friesian cows to average more than 18 litres daily over their whole lactation without any assistance from concentrates. If the price of the latter is high in relation to milk prices, we may be forced into very low-level concentrate feeding, and if this is so, then concentrates should be fed early in lactation when a cow is at her peak of efficiency in converting nutrients into milk, rather than after her peak when additional feeding tends to put fat on her back rather than milk in the bucket.

We cannot be categoric about the optimal time for calving cows. We suggest about six weeks in advance of active pasture growth as being a suitable time, but in the more favoured pastoral areas such as Pembrokeshire or County Cork it may be preferable to reduce this interval to a month and thereby effect economies in the conservation programme along the lines adopted by New Zealand dairy farmers. Calving in April, in our experience, is too late because we find that though these late calving cows have a good peak yield, they have a fore-shortened lactation. The aim at Frondeg Farm has been to complete calving by the beginning of February and in most years this has been substantially achieved.

WINTER MILK PRODUCTION

We are not, because of our special interest in this topic, advocating a wholesale move to summer milk production, since, for obvious reasons, winter milk production will continue to be an important feature of British dairying for many years to come. What we are suggesting is that any expansion of the industry as a consequence of a greater demand for manufacturing milk should mainly be in the summer production category, especially in those parts of the country that are well suited to this approach. The great majority of British dairy farmers, however, will still be concerned with the problems of producing winter milk as efficiently as possible in the face of rising costs, especially those for land, labour, and purchased feeding stuffs.

There are two features of the Frondeg Farm project which are of considerable importance to winter milk producers as well as to those whose emphasis is on summer milk. The first is the importance of growing heifers so that they can safely calve for the first time at two years of age. Among other things this reduces the amount of nutriment that has to be devoted to followers at the expense of a larger milking herd. Also there are but two very uniform groups, rising yearlings and rising two-year-old heifers and this simplifies management, particularly when stock are at pasture.

The second feature is that as a result of the very tight control of the calving pattern all the cows are dry over a period of about six weeks, coinciding with the shortest days of the year when routine chores are reduced to a minimum and there is no necessity for an early start to the working day. With the increasing pressures on dairy farm labour and the higher physical contributions that farmers and members of their family have to make to the handling of dairy herds a respite of this nature has much to commend it. Admittedly, it is more difficult to effect a tight calving pattern in the autumn to give a summer break but as many farmers have demonstrated it can be achieved by careful attention to mating management and especially to ensuring that cows are not losing condition at time of service.

Chapter 20

PROGRESS IN GRASSLAND HUSBANDRY

NATURE OF GRASSLAND RESEARCH

Looking at the development of grassland husbandry over the past 50 years, not only in Great Britain but in other humid temperate countries as well, quite a remarkable feature has been the substantial contributions made by practising farmers towards the greater efficiency of pasture utilisation. This does not deny the important part played by agricultural scientists, in particular plant breeders who by selection of more productive ecotypes and, subsequently, by purposeful genetic manipulation have vastly improved the quality of herbage seeds, and the grassland ecologists who have provided a better understanding of the dynamics of grassland associations and how those can be managed to the best advantage.

However, pasture differs from cash crops in that except for seed production it is primarily a means to an end rather than an end in itself. A crop agronomist can, with a comparatively small area of land and in very few years, demonstrate effectively a combination of factors that will give the optimal performance of a crop such as potatoes or wheat. His counterpart in pasture agronomy can only go so far with a crop of grass; for instance, he can establish and control to some extent the factors that influence the production of dry matter over the course of the year but seldom does he have the resources to take the ultimate step of harvesting and measuring the worth of herbage in terms of milk or meat.

In this respect British agricultural scientists have been at something of a disadvantage as compared with those in New Zealand and Australia where small plot experimentation is only part of the total grassland research effort and the 'whole farm' approach makes an important contribution to the output of research centres. Several references made in previous chapters to results coming from Ruakura in New Zealand illustrate this point. The late C. P. McMeekan who was Director of Ruakura in the post-war years of its expansion, and undoubtedly in his time one of the world's leading thinkers in agriculture, was a firm believer in trying to answer the farmers' problems with a farmer's approach. Fortunately he and his associates had the land and the livestock and, equally important, the confidence, because many of them were of farming stock, to tackle such areas as grazing systems, rearing regimes in relation to life-time performance, stocking intensities, and choice of animal and their effect on individual performance and output per unit area. He devised alternative farm models that were tested under realistic farming conditions to constitute meaningful comparisons in the estimation of the general body of farmers who came to Ruakura in thousands on open days.

With McMeekan's dynamic and sometimes provocative approach Ruakura became a Mecca not just for New Zealand farmers but also for visitors from abroad, not only research workers but also farmers, many of them from Britain and Eire. It was not uncommon to hear progressive farmers like Wilfrid Cave, John Cherrington and Rex Paterson, after visits to New Zealand, asking why British grassland research centres did not manifest the same sort of practical commitment to farmers' problems that they had seen in New Zealand not only at Ruakura but at Massey and Lincoln as well.

This is not the context for discussing this matter beyond making the point that New Zealand is primarily a farming country and agricultural research workers are generally much more identified with the countryside and its problems than they are in Britain. Moreover, the land and livestock resources are more freely available there than they are in this country. Significantly in Eire, another primarily agricultural country, the position is more like that in New Zealand and over the last two decades the Irish Agricultural Institute has established the importance of its role in the farming of that country. Moore Park in dairy productioin and the Grange, which is primarily concerned with beef cattle, both have the confidence of farmers and their contributions to a more effective realisation of Eire's grassland potential are substantial.

CONTRIBUTIONS FROM FARMERS

Fortunately in Britain the development gap between research on the one hand and farming practice on the other has been spanned and manned with great success by a band of progressive farmers, cither working independently or in some instances with the help of field staff from fertiliser firms such as ICI and Fisons, particularly in respect of performance recording. Apart from Government-financed advisory and development services, organisations like the Meat and Livestock Commission and the Farm Management Services of the English Milk Marketing Board have collected and interpreted data from surveys relating to meat and dairy production with a particular emphasis on efficiency of land and grassland utilisation.

The British Grassland Society, which was Stapledon's brain child, has not only provided a common forum for both farmers and research workers but through its encouragement of county grassland societies has strengthened the links between research and development, with leading farmers making very significant contributions in this latter area. We have already mentioned several of these grassland farming pioneers in preceding chapters in particular Rex Paterson who was the first farmer to become President of the British Grassland Society. Apart from his innovations of the buckrake, the fertiliser spinner and the self-feeding of silage, his system of grassland recording on the large number of dairy farms he operated gave a meaningful comparison of a range of pasture combinations. More than anyone else he established the fallacy of attributing a gallon of milk to every 4 lbs of concentrates that were fed to dairy cows, making the grass component the residuary legatee of all the errors of this erroneous calculation. The so-called Utilised Starch Equivalent figures, that had some temporary support as a measure of grassland productivity that was calculated on this basis, failed because it did not give full credit to either pasture or forage crops.

Another more recent President of the BGS, who is also an outstanding farmer, is Edwin Bushby of Watson Hill, near Egremont in Cumbria. Thirty years ago this 50-hectare holding carried about 40 Northern Dairy Shorthorn cows with no more than average yields for that breed. Progressively he has lifted carrying capacity by over 250 per cent and average milk sales are well in excess of 7,000 litres per cow and 12,000 litres per hectare with a concentrate usage of only 0·2 kg/litre. His farming, which has been an example to dairy farmers throughout Britain, exemplifies to a high degree the operation and integration of the factors that are important in grassland production and utilisation – a liberal use of fertilisers, controlled grazing, judicious use of concentrates, an emphasis on silage quality, a high level of stockmanship and a herd of very high genetic merit as a result of nominated matings.

Another stalwart in a different branch of grassland utilisation is Fenwick Jackson of Shoreswood in North Northumberland, who from 1956 onwards did more than anyone else to establish the production of beef based on dairy-bred calves which is now commonly referred to as the eighteen-month system. His brother Edward, near Alnwick, is currently demonstrating the components of a successful system of intensive fat lamb production. The important factors are the scrupulous maintenance of field hygiene combined with strategic dosing for worms, the use of protective vaccines, a flock of inherently prolific ewes which are mated in prime condition to maximise the lamb crop, inwintering not only to protect pastures which receive generous fertiliser applications, but also to reduce neo-natal losses, and a judicious use of concentrates. The whole constitute a carefully devised and integrated system that profits from the advances in basic knowledge made over the past 30 years.

Men like the Jacksons and Edwin Bushby and other grassland progressives have sons, many with formal educations in agriculture and therefore with a knowledge of the basic biology of their calling and they are gradually taking over from their fathers. As a result there can be no other expectation than a continued improvement in the off-take of animal products from grassland, not only in this country but also abroad. It will be part of a continuous process in Britain which had its genesis in the depths of the agricultural depression of the thirties when George Stapledon first sowed seeds of hope that have continued to bear fruit. Certainly pastoral farming in Britain has come a very long way since 1949 when the senior author created a sense of national outrage when he asserted in a paper given to the British Association for the Advancement of Science that British farming, despite all the war time efforts, was still only at half cock. In the subsequent 30 years leading British farmers have established by their efforts the validity of this criticism as far as grassland farming is concerned.

Index